WHAT THE WORLD'S GREATEST FINANCIAL LEADERS ARE SAYING ABOUT TONY ROBBINS . . .

"Remarkably, Robbins has produced a book that will appeal to both the beginner and the most sophisticated money jockey overseeing multibillions of dollars in assets. If there were a Pulitzer Prize for investment books, this one would win, hands down."

> —Steve Forbes, publisher of *Forbes* magazine and CEO of Forbes Inc.

"Robbins is the best economic moderator that I've ever worked with. His mission to bring insights from the world's greatest financial minds to the average investor is truly inspiring."

> —Alan Greenspan, former Federal Reserve chairman
> under four sitting presidents

"Tony came to my office for a 45-minute interview that ended up lasting four hours. It was one of the most wide-ranging and probing interviews I've done in my 65-year career in the mutual fund industry. Tony's energy and passion are contagious and energizing; I knew right away his book would have a huge impact on investors."

> —John C. Bogle, founder, the Vanguard Group,
> which has over $3 trillion in assets under management

"In this book, Tony Robbins brings his unique talent for making the complex simple as he distills the concepts of the best investors in the world into practical lessons that will benefit both naïve investors and skilled professionals."

—Ray Dalio, founder and co–chief investment officer, Bridgewater Associates, and the #1 hedge fund investor in the world

"Tony Robbins needs no introduction. He is committed to helping make life better for every investor. Every investor will find this book extremely interesting and illuminating."

—Carl Icahn, billionaire activist investor

"You can't meet Tony Robbins and listen to his words without being inspired to act. This book will give you the strategies to create financial freedom for yourself and your family."

—T. Boone Pickens, founder, chairman, and CEO of BP Capital Management and TBP Investments Management; predicted oil prices accurately 18 out of 21 times on CNBC

"Tony masterfully weaves anecdote and expertise to simplify the process of investing for readers—priming their financial education and helping them effectively plan for their future."

—Mary Callahan Erdoes, CEO, JPMorgan Asset Management; $2.4 trillion in assets under management

"Tony Robbins is a human locksmith—he knows how to open your mind to larger possibilities. Using his unique insights into human nature, he's found a way to simplify the strategies of the world's greatest investors so that anyone can have the financial freedom they deserve."

—Paul Tudor Jones II, founder, Tudor Investment Corporation, and one of the top ten traders in history

"Robbins' unrelenting commitment to finding the real answers to financial security and independence, and his passion for bringing the insights of the ultrawealthy to the average man, is truly inspiring. This book could truly change your life."

—David Pottruck, former CEO of Charles Schwab
Corporation and bestselling author of *Stacking the Deck:
How to Lead Breakthrough Change Against Any Odds*

"Tony Robbins has influenced millions of people's lives, including my own. In this book, he offers you insights and strategies from the world's greatest investors. Don't miss the opportunity to experience the life-changing value of this book."

—Kyle Bass, founder of Hayman Capital Management and investor who
turned $30 million into $2 billion in the middle of the subprime crisis

"It's rare that an outsider steals the spotlight and becomes a respected voice of impact in the financial industry. Robbins does it again with a new book to prepare us and help us profit from the inevitable crashes and corrections to come."

—Anthony Scaramucci, founder, SkyBridge Capital;
cohost of *Wall Street Week*

WHAT LEADERS FROM OTHER INDUSTRIES ARE SAYING ABOUT TONY ROBBINS . . .

"He has a great gift. He has the gift to inspire."
—Bill Clinton, former president of the United States

"Tony's power is superhuman. . . . He is a catalyst for getting people to change."
—Oprah Winfrey, Emmy Award–winning media magnate

"We've been selected by *Forbes* as the most innovative company in the world for four consecutive years. Our revenues are now over $7 billion annually. Without access to Tony and his teachings, Salesforce.com wouldn't exist today."
—Marc Benioff, founder, chairman, and CEO of Salesforce.com

"Tony Robbins' coaching has made a remarkable difference in my life both on and off the court. He's helped me discover what I'm really made of, and I've taken my tennis game—and my life—to a whole new level!"
—Serena Williams, 22-time Grand Slam tennis champion and Olympic gold medalist

"I was afraid that my success would take something away from my family. Tony was able to turn it around and show me that I've helped millions of people. Probably the most intense feelings I've ever had."
—Melissa Etheridge, two-time Grammy Award–winning singer and songwriter

"No matter who you are, no matter how successful, no matter how happy, Tony has something to offer you."

—Hugh Jackman, Emmy– and Tony Award–winning actor and producer

"If you want to change your state, if you want to change your results, this is where you do it: Tony is the man."

—Usher, Grammy Award–winning singer, songwriter, entrepreneur

"What Tony really gave me, a kid sitting on Venice Beach selling T-shirts, was to take risks, take action, and really become something. I'm telling you as someone who has lived with these strategies for 25 years: I'll come back for more again and again and again."

—Mark Burnett, five-time Emmy Award–winning television producer

"What does this man have that everyone wants? He is a six-foot-seven phenomenon!"

—Diane Sawyer, former *ABC World News* and *Good Morning America* anchor

UNSHAKEABLE
YOUR FINANCIAL FREEDOM PLAYBOOK

TONY ROBBINS
with PETER MALLOUK

SIMON & SCHUSTER PAPERBACKS

NEW YORK LONDON TORONTO SYDNEY NEW DELHI

Simon & Schuster Paperbacks
A Division of Simon & Schuster, Inc.
1230 Avenue of the Americas
New York, NY 10020

Copyright © 2017 by Tony Robbins

First Simon & Schuster trade paperback edition September 2018

SIMON & SCHUSTER PAPERBACKS and colophon are registered trademarks
of Simon & Schuster, Inc.

For information about special discounts for bulk purchases, please contact
Simon & Schuster Special Sales at 1-866-506-1949
or business@simonandschuster.com.

The Simon & Schuster Speakers Bureau can bring authors to your
live event. For more information or to book an event, contact the
Simon & Schuster Speakers Bureau at 1-866-248-3049
or visit our website at www.simonspeakers.com.

Interior design by Paul Dippolito

Cover Photo by Joseph Seif

Manufactured in the United States of America

10 9 8 7 6 5 4 3

Library of Congress Cataloging-in-Publication Data is available.

ISBN 978-1-5011-6458-3
ISBN 978-1-5011-6459-0 (pbk)
ISBN 978-1-5011-6460-6 (ebook)

To those souls who will never settle for less than they can be, do, share, and give

CONTENTS

SECTION III

THE PSYCHOLOGY OF WEALTH

Waste no more time arguing about
what a good man should be.
Be one.
—MARCUS AURELIUS

Money is only a tool.
It will take you wherever you wish,
but it will not replace you as the driver.
—AYN RAND

INTRODUCTION

Steve Forbes, publisher of Forbes *magazine and CEO of Forbes Inc.*

This short, wisdom-rich, and crisply written book couldn't be more timely. Even better, its insights and recommendations are timeless. Investors and, more important, those who currently are not investing should read it and take what it says to heart.

Never have we had such a long bull market that has been accompanied from the beginning by such caution and outright pessimism about the durability of the rise. The stock market never goes in a straight line, up or down, and every dip it has taken since 2009 has been met with wails of woe that we are in for another horrific slide. A result of this aversion to investing is that tens of millions of people who should be in the market, particularly millennials, are not. Tony Robbins aptly points out that regarding the accumulation of assets, especially for retirement, they are making a very costly long-term mistake by staying on the sidelines.

What helps make this volume so credible is that the author is up front in dealing with the pervasive anxieties about our economic future, worries that made the 2016 election cycle so stunning. He acknowledges that, yes, eventually we will experience a real bear market. But the possibility of such an event is no reason for individuals to stay away and simply sit on their hands. Big downturns in the market happen periodically, but the long-term trend of stocks has *always* been upward. By taking to heart the truth that emotions are enemy number one when it comes to investing, individuals can devise strategies that will enable them to outperform the market *and* most professional managers.

Robbins carefully and thoughtfully shows how you can be the master of your investment fate instead of sitting fearfully on the sidelines or getting whipsawed by reacting to market volatility in panicky, damaging ways. **What should you do when stocks plummet? How can you find opportunity when everyone else sees disaster?** He provides sensible rules that will keep you from making costly mistakes and, even better, explains what actions to take—such as recalibrating your allocation of assets—that can lay the foundation for fulsome future returns.

Enemy number two is fees. Expenses come not only from advertised costs but also from a variety of hidden charges. Thanks to compounding, these outlays over time can literally reduce your nest egg by hundreds of thousands of dollars. Remember that each dollar in expenses means one less dollar that can grow in coming years. This is why you should take a careful look at your 401(k) to discover what exactions might be eating away at it, like termites do with a house. Even index funds can hit you with unnecessary charges. As for a popular investment instrument, annuities, their charges can do to your money what Godzilla did to cities. An informed investor will be a far richer investor.

A lot of regulatory changes are taking place in the world of managing money, most notably from the US Department of Labor (DOL). This book helpfully walks you through these.

Finally, Robbins makes the point that wealth creation is not an end in and of itself but is a crucial aspect of achieving a purposeful life, a truth too often ignored. My grandfather B. C. Forbes, who founded our company just about a century ago, observed in the first issue of the magazine that bears his name that "the purpose of business is to produce happiness, not to pile up money."

We can hope only that more people, especially the younger ones just starting their working careers, will take Robbins's investment message to heart: get in!

He's right. Millennials are making the same mistake a previous generation made decades ago—a generation that was scarred by the catastrophe of the Great Depression. Those folks' fear of stocks was all too understandable. From 1929 to 1932, the Dow Jones Industrial Average went down what today would be the equivalent of 17,000 points! That's a plunge of almost 90%. The 1930s was plagued by high unemployment. Then came World War II. No wonder most Americans vowed never to go near a stock.

Yet after WWII, the United States entered a great period of prosperity. Stock prices went up manyfold. Sadly, all too many people stayed out or overinvested in seemingly safe bonds; they could hardly know that the debt market was starting what turned out to be a 35-year bear market. Investors lost staggering sums to the inflation that pummeled the bonds' principle. These people missed out on a fantastic opportunity to enrich their lives.

So never forget about these two ferocious foes of stock market success: fear and fees.

Will this sage book make Tony Robbins rich? No. All the proceeds are going to Feeding America, which provides free meals to those who need them. In this, Robbins exemplifies a basic truth that is often ignored: commerce and philanthropy are not polar opposites; they are two sides of the same coin. In free markets, you succeed only by providing a product or service that others want—that is, you prosper by meeting the needs and wants of others. Philanthropy is about meeting the needs of others. The skill sets required in each of these spheres may differ, but the fundamental objective is the same. In fact, successful businesspeople often become successful philanthropists. Bill Gates is only one example of many.

Tony Robbins demonstrates that by creating resources, by producing something, you gain the means to help others. His book will be your invaluable guide to enabling you to do the same—and on a scale you may never have thought possible.

FOREWORD

*John C. Bogle, founder of Vanguard, which has
more than $3 trillion in assets under management*

As 2016 began, I started my Saturday morning reading the *New York Times* while eating breakfast. After scanning the front page (and pulling out the crossword puzzle for later), I turned my attention to the business section. Displayed prominently at the top of section B1 was Ron Lieber's Your Money column, which featured essential money management strategies written on index cards by six personal finance experts.

Ron's point was to show that effective money management does not need to be complicated, with the key points of managing your money fitting on a single index card. Five out of the six index cards addressed the topic of how to invest your savings, and each gave the same simple advice: invest in index funds.

That message is getting through to investors. In 1975 I created the world's first index mutual fund, and I've been singing its praises ever since. In those early days, I was a lone voice without much of an audience. Today an enormous choir has developed to help me spread the word. Investors are hearing our voices loud and clear, and are voting with their feet—in other words, their dollars.

Since the end of 2007, mutual fund investors have added almost $1.65 trillion to their holdings of equity index funds while reducing their holdings of actively managed mutual funds by $750 billion. That swing of $2.4 trillion in investor preferences over the last nine years is, I believe, unprecedented in the history of the mutual fund industry.

Over the past seven years, Tony Robbins has been on a mission to help the average investor win the game, preach the message of index funds, and tell investors to stop overpaying for underperformance. In his journey, he has spoken to some of the greatest minds in finance. Although I'm not sure I belong in that category, Tony came to my office at Vanguard to get my thoughts on investing. Let me tell you, Tony is a force of nature! After spending just a few minutes with Tony, I completely understand how he's been able to inspire millions of people all over the world.

We had such a great time speaking with each other that our scheduled 45-minute interview ended up lasting four hours. It was one of the most wide-ranging and probing interviews I've done in my 65-year career in the mutual fund industry. Tony's energy and passion are contagious and energizing; I knew right away his book would have a huge impact on investors.

But even I underestimated just how big an impact Tony would have. His first book on investing, *Money: Master the Game*, has sold over one million copies and spent seven months at the top of the *New York Times* Business Best Sellers list. Now he returns with *Unshakeable*, which is sure to add even more value to readers. *Unshakeable* presents insights from some of the most important figures in the investing world, such as Warren Buffett and Yale endowment fund manager David Swensen. Both Warren and David have said time and again that index funds are the best way for investors to maximize their chances of investment success. This book will help that message reach even more investors.

Index funds are simple. Rather than try to time the market or outguess other professional money managers about the prospects of individual stocks, index funds simply buy and hold all of the stocks in a broad market index such as the S&P 500. Index funds work by paring the costs of investing to the bare-bones minimum. They pay no fees to expensive money managers and have minimal trading costs, as they follow the ultimate buy-and-hold strategy. We can't control what the markets will do, but we can control how much we pay for our investments. Index funds allow you to invest, at minimal cost, in a portfolio diversified to the nth degree.

Think about it this way: all investors as a group own the market and therefore share the market's gross return (before costs). By simply owning the entire market, index funds also earn the market's return at minimal annual cost: as low as 0.05% of the amount you invest. The rest of the market is active, with investors and money managers furiously trading back and forth with one another, trying to outperform the market. Yet they too, as a group, own the entire market and earn the market's gross return. All of that trading is enormously expensive. The fund managers demand (and receive) huge fees, while Wall Street takes a cut from all that frenzied trading. These and other hidden fees can easily add up to over 2% each year.

So index fund investors receive the gross market return minus fees as low as 0.05% or less, while active investors as a group will receive the same gross return minus 2% or more. *The gross return of the market minus the cost of investing equals the net return to investors.* This "cost matters hypothesis" is all you need to know to understand the benefits of index investing. Over an investment lifetime, this annual difference really adds up. Most young people just starting their careers will be investing for 60 years or more. **Compounded over that time frame, the high costs of investing can confiscate an astounding 70% of your lifetime returns!**

This cost differential substantially *understates* the costs incurred by so many investors—especially investors in 403(b) and 401(k) retirement plans. As Tony points out in chapter 3, this extra layer of fees (often largely hidden) confiscates an additional staggering proportion of the returns delivered by your funds.

I'm excited to add my small contribution to this book and support Tony in being a voice for good. I'm thrilled to have spent a wonderful afternoon conversing with him. I'm humbled to have the opportunity to spread the gospel of indexing, to help the honest-to-God, down-to-earth human beings who are saving for a secure retirement or for their children's education.

With flair and depth, Tony covers the history of investment risks and returns, and successful investors should understand this history. That said, history, as the British poet Samuel Taylor Coleridge wrote, is but "a lantern on the stern, which shines only on the waves behind us," and not on where we are headed. The past is not necessarily prologue to the future.

We live in an uncertain world, and face not only the risks of the known unknowns but also the unknown unknowns: the ones that "we don't know we don't know." Despite these risks, if we are to have any chance for meeting our long-term financial goals, invest we must. Otherwise we're certain to fall short. But we don't have to put up 100% of the capital and take 100% of the risk only to receive 30% of the reward (often far less). By buying low-cost, broad-market index funds (and holding them "forever"), you can guarantee that you will receive your fair share of whatever returns the financial markets provide over the long term.

WEALTH: THE RULE BOOK

CHAPTER 1

UNSHAKEABLE

Power and Peace of Mind in a World of Uncertainty

un·shake·able
An unwavering and undisputed confidence;
a steadfast commitment to the truth;
presence, peace of mind, and a calm amidst the storm

What would it feel like to know in your mind, in your heart, and in the very depth of your soul that you'll always be prosperous? To know with absolute certainty that no matter what happens in the economy, stock market, or real estate, you'll have financial security for the rest of your life? To know that you'll possess an abundance that will enable you not only to take care of your family's needs but also to delight in the joy of helping others?

We all dream of achieving that tremendous inner peace, that comfort, that independence, that freedom. **In short, we all dream of being unshakeable.**

But what does it really mean to be unshakeable?

It's not just a matter of money. It's a state of mind. **When you're truly unshakeable, you have unwavering confidence even amidst the storm**. It's not that nothing upsets you. We can all get hooked. But you don't stay there. Nothing rattles you for any length of time. You don't allow fear to take you over. If you're knocked off balance, you find your center quickly and regain your inner calm. When others are afraid, you have the presence of mind to take advantage of the turmoil swirling all around you. This state of mind allows you to be a *leader*, not a follower. To be the chess *player*, not the chess piece. To be one of the few who *do*, not one of the many who merely talk!

But is it even *possible* to become unshakeable in these crazy times? Or is it just a pipe dream?

Do you remember how you felt in 2008 when the financial crisis savaged the global economy? Do you remember the fear, the anxiety, the uncertainty that gripped us all when the world seemed to be falling apart? The stock market collapsed, maybe crushing your 401(k). The property market was beaten to a pulp, maybe wrecking the value of your home or that of some-one you love. Big banks fell over like toy soldiers. Millions of good, hard-working people lost their jobs.

I can tell you right now, I'll never forget the suffering and terror I wit-nessed all around me. I saw people lose their life savings, get kicked out of their homes, and not have the money to send their kids to college. My bar-ber told me that his business was in tatters because people didn't even want to spend money getting their hair cut. Even some of my billionaire clients called me in a panic because their cash was all tied up, the credit markets had frozen, and it suddenly looked like they might be in danger of losing ev-erything. Fear was like a virus, spreading everywhere. It began to take over people's lives, infecting millions with a sense of total uncertainty.

Wouldn't it be wonderful if all that uncertainty had ended in 2008? Didn't you think the world would be back to normal by now? That the global economy would be back on track and growing dynamically again?

But the truth is, we're *still* living in a crazy world. All these years later, central bankers are *still* fighting an epic battle to revive economic growth. They're *still* experimenting with radical policies that we've never seen in the entire history of the global economy.

You think I'm exaggerating? Well, think again. First-world countries such as Switzerland, Sweden, Germany, Denmark, and Japan now have "negative" interest rates. You know how insane that is? The whole purpose of the banking system is for you to make a profit by loaning money to banks, so they can lend it out to others. But people around the world now have to *pay* banks to accept their hard-earned savings. The *Wall Street Jour-nal* wanted to discover when the world *last* experienced a period of negative yields. So the newspaper called an economic historian. You know what he told them? It's the first time this has happened in 5,000 years of banking history.

That's how far we've come from living in a normal world: borrowers get paid to borrow, and savers get punished for saving. In this upside-down environment, "safe" investments such as high-quality bonds offer such terrible returns that you wonder if someone's having a laugh at your expense. I recently learned that the finance arm of Toyota had issued a three-year bond that yields just 0.001%. At that rate, it would take you 69,300 years to double your money!

If you're struggling to make sense of what all this means for the future of the global economy, join the club. Howard Marks, a legendary investor who oversees nearly $100 billion in assets, recently told me, "If you're not confused, you don't understand what's going on."

You know we're living in strange times when even the greatest financial minds admit to being confused. For me, this reality was driven home emphatically last year when I arranged a meeting of my Platinum Partners: an intimate group of friends and clients who gather once a year to gain financial insights from the best of the best.

We had already listened to the opinions of seven self-made billionaires. But now it was time to hear from a man who, for two decades, had wielded more economic power than anyone else alive. I was seated in one of two leather wingback chairs on a stage in a conference room at the Four Seasons hotel in Whistler, British Columbia. Outside the snow was falling gently. The man sitting across from me was none other than Alan Greenspan, former chairman of the US Federal Reserve. Appointed by President Ronald Reagan in 1987, Greenspan ultimately served as the Fed chief to *four* presidents before retiring in 2006. We could hardly have asked for a more experienced insider to cut through the confusion and shed light on the future of the economy.

As our two-hour conversation drew to a close, I had one final question for this man who had seen it all, who had guided the US economy through thick and thin for 19 years. "Alan, you've had 90 years on this planet and have seen incredible changes in the world economy," I began. "So, in this world of intense volatility and insane central banking policies around the globe, what is the one thing you would do if you were still the Fed chairman today?"

Greenspan paused for a while. Finally, he leaned forward and said: "*Resign!*"

HOW TO FIND CERTAINTY IN
AN UNCERTAIN TIME

What are you supposed to do when even an economic icon of Alan Greenspan's stature is tempted to throw up his hands in dismay, unable to make sense of what's going on or guess where it will end? If *he* can't figure it out, how on earth can you and I predict what will happen?

If you're feeling stressed and confused, I understand. **But let me tell you the good news: there are a few people who *do* have the answers—a few brilliant financial minds that have figured out how to make money in good times and bad.** After spending seven years interviewing these masters of the financial game, I'm going to bring you their answers, their insights, their secrets, so you can understand how to win even in these incredibly uncertain times.

And I'll tell you this: one of the greatest lessons I've learned from these money masters is that you don't have to predict the future to win this game. Etch that idea into your big, beautiful brain, because it's important. Really important.

Here's what you *do* have to do: you have to focus on what you *can* control, not on what you can't. You can't control where the economy is headed and whether the stock market will soar or plunge. But that doesn't matter! The winners of the financial game know that *they* can't control the future, either. They know their predictions will often be wrong because the world is just too complex and fast changing for anybody to foresee the future. But, as you'll learn in the pages to come, they focus so intently on what they *can* control that they'll thrive no matter what happens to the economy or the financial markets. And with the help of their insights, you'll thrive, too.

Control what you can control. That's the trick. And this book will show you exactly how to do it. Above all, you'll finish the book with a strategic plan that provides you the tools to help you win the game.

We all know that we're *not* going to become unshakeable through wishful thinking, or by lying to ourselves, or by merely thinking positive, or by putting photos of exotic cars on our "vision boards." It's not enough to believe. You need the insights, the tools, the skills, the expertise, and the *specific strategies* that will empower you to achieve true and lasting prosperity. **You need to learn the rules of the financial game, who the players are, what their agendas are, where you can get hurt, and how you can win. This knowledge can set you free**.

The big purpose of this small book is to provide you with that essential knowledge. It will give you a complete playbook for financial success, so that you and your family won't ever again have to live in fear and uncertainty but can enjoy the journey with true peace of mind.

Many people just dabble in and out when it comes to their financial lives, and they pay an enormous price for it. That's not because they don't care. It's because they get swamped by all the stresses and strains of their daily lives. Plus, they don't have expertise in this area, so it seems intimidating, confusing, and overwhelming. None of us likes putting effort into things that make us feel unsuccessful and out of our depth! When people are forced to make financial decisions, they often act out of fear—and any decision made in a state of fear is likely to be wrong.

But my commitment here is to be your coach, to guide you and help you, so you can put together an action plan that gets you from where you are today to where you *want* to be. Maybe you're a baby boomer who worries that you can't get to financial security because you started too late. Maybe you're a millennial who thinks, "I've got so much debt, I'll never be free." Maybe you're a sophisticated investor who's looking for an edge so you can build a legacy that benefits generations to come. Whoever you are and whatever stage of life you're at, I'm here to show you that there *is* a way.

If you commit to stay with me through the pages of this book, I promise to provide you with the knowledge and tools you need to get the job done. Once you absorb this information and put your plan in place, it will likely take you only an hour or two each year to keep things on target.

This is an area of life that requires commitment. But if you're committed to understanding and harnessing the insights in this book, the rewards will be incredible. How much stronger and more confident will you feel when you know the rules that govern the financial world? When you have that knowledge, that *mastery*, then you can make smart financial decisions based on real understanding. And decisions are the ultimate power. **Decisions**

equal destiny. The decisions you will be equipped to make after reading this short book can bring you a whole new level of inner peace, fulfillment, comfort, and financial freedom that most humans only dream of achieving. I know that sounds like hyperbole. But as you'll discover for yourself, it's not.

MEET THE MONEY MASTERS

My life's obsession is to help people create the life of their dreams. My greatest pleasure is to show them how to rise from pain to power. I can't bear to see others suffer, because I know how it feels. I grew up dirt poor, with four different fathers over the years, and with a mother who was an alcoholic. I often went to bed hungry, not knowing if there'd be anything to eat the next day. We had so little money that I bought T-shirts for 25 cents at the thrift store and went to high school in Levi's cords that were four inches too short for me. To support myself, I worked as a janitor at two banks in the middle of the night, and then caught a bus home and slept for roughly four to five hours before dragging myself back to school each morning.

Today I'm blessed with financial success. But I can tell you right now, I'll never forget what it was like to live in that state of constant anxiety about the future. In those days, I was trapped by my circumstances and filled with uncertainty. So when I saw what happened to people during the 2008–09 financial crisis, there was no way I could turn my back on them.

What drove me crazy was that much of that economic mayhem had been caused by the reckless ways of a small minority of bad actors on Wall Street. Yet nobody in a position of power and privilege seemed to pay any price for the pain that was created. Nobody went to jail. Nobody addressed the systemic issues that had made the economy so vulnerable in the first place. Nobody seemed to be looking out for the regular people who bore the brunt of this financial chaos. I saw them getting used and abused every day, and I couldn't take it anymore.

That launched me on a quest to figure out how I could help people to gain control over their financial lives so they'd never again be passive victims of a game they didn't understand. I had one key advantage: personal access to many of the giants of the financial world. It helped that I've coached

Paul Tudor Jones, one of the greatest traders of all time. Paul, an extraordinary philanthropist, a brilliant thinker, and a dear friend, helped to open a lot of doors for me.

Over seven years, I interviewed more than 50 masters of the financial universe. Their names may mean nothing to you. But in the financial world, these guys have the star power and the name recognition of celebrities such as LeBron James, Robert De Niro, Jay Z, and Beyoncé!

The list of legends who ended up sharing their insights with me includes Ray Dalio, the most successful hedge fund manager in history; Jack Bogle, the founder of Vanguard and the revered pioneer of index funds; Mary Callahan Erdoes, who oversees $2.4 trillion in assets at JPMorgan Chase & Co.; T. Boone Pickens, the billionaire oil tycoon; Carl Icahn, America's most formidable "activist" investor; David Swensen, whose financial wizardry transformed Yale into one of the world's wealthiest universities; John Paulson, a hedge fund manager who personally earned $4.9 billion in 2010; and Warren Buffett, the most celebrated investor ever to walk the earth.

If you don't know these names, you're not alone. Unless you work in finance, you're probably more aware of how your fantasy football team is doing or what's in your Net-a-Porter shopping cart. But you're really going to want these financial titans to be on your radar, too, because they can literally change your life.

The result of all that research was my 670-page behemoth of a book, *Money: Master the Game*. To my delight, it skyrocketed to number one on the *New York Times* Business Best Sellers list and has sold more than a million copies since its publication in 2014. The book has also received an extraordinary array of endorsements from the financial elite. Carl Icahn, not an easy man to win over, declared, "Every investor will find this book extremely interesting and illuminating." Jack Bogle wrote, "This book will enlighten you and reinforce your understanding of how to master the money game and, in the long run, earn your financial freedom." Steve Forbes wrote, "If there were a Pulitzer Prize for investment books, this one would win, hands down."

I'd like to think this praise was a testament to my literary brilliance! But the success of *Money: Master the Game* really reflects the generosity of all those financial giants in sitting down with me for hours on end and sharing their knowledge. Anyone who takes the time to study and apply what they told me should attain huge financial rewards that can last a lifetime.

So why bother to write a *second* book on how to achieve your financial ambitions? After all, there are plenty of easier and more painless ways to spend my time than writing books. Like, say, selling my organs on the black market. But, my goal is to empower you, the reader, while also making a difference for millions of forgotten people who are in desperate need.

I've donated all my profits from *Money: Master the Game* and now for this book, *Unshakeable*, to provide free meals for the hungry through my partnership with Feeding America, the nation's most effective charity for feeding the hungry. So far, between these books and the additional personal donations I've made over the last two years, we've provided over 250 million free meals to families in need. In the next eight years, I plan to bring that total to a billion meals. If you're holding this book, you've contributed to that cause. Thanks! And feel free to buy copies for all your friends and family!

Beyond that mission, I have three urgent reasons for writing *Unshakeable*. First, I want to reach as many people as possible by writing a short book that you can read in a couple of evenings or a weekend. If you want to go deeper, I hope you'll also read *Money: Master the Game*, but I understand if that big monster seems intimidating. **Unshakeable is designed to be a concise companion that contains all of the essential facts and strategies you need to transform your financial life.**

In writing a short book that's quick and easy to read, I'm looking to increase the likelihood that you'll not only master this material but also *act* on it. People love to say that knowledge is power. But the truth is that knowledge is only *potential* power. You and I both know that it's useless if you don't act on it. This book gives you a power-packed action plan that you can put into effect immediately—because execution trumps knowledge every day of the week.

My second reason for writing *Unshakeable* is that I see so much fear around me today. How are you and I going to make smart, rational financial decisions if we're full of fear? Even if you *know* what to do, fear keeps you from doing it. I'm concerned that you might make the wrong moves if you're fearful, damaging yourself and your family in ways that I believe are entirely avoidable. Step-by-step, this book will enable you to systematically free yourself from that fear.

BABY, IT'S COLD OUTSIDE!

As I write this, the stock market has risen for seven and a half years in a row, making this the second-longest bull market in US history. There's a widespread sense that we're due for a fall, that what goes up must come down, that winter is coming. By the time you read this, the market may already have tumbled. But, as we'll discuss in the next chapter, the truth is that nobody—I repeat, *nobody*—can accurately predict with any consistency where the financial markets are headed. That includes all those smooth-talking TV pundits, those Wall Street economists in pinstripe suits, and all those other high-paid purveyors of snake oil.

We all know that winter is coming, that the stock market will fall again. But none of us knows *when* winter is coming or how *severe* it will be. Does that mean we're powerless? Not at all. **Unshakeable will show you how the masters of the financial world prepare themselves—how they profit by *anticipating* winter instead of just *reacting* to it. As a result, you'll be able to benefit from the very thing that harms those who are unprepared**. Ask yourself this: When an ice storm comes, do you want to be the one who's stuck outside, freezing in the bitter cold? Or do you want to be the one who's wrapped up warmly by the fire, toasting marshmallows?

Let me give you a recent example of how it pays to be prepared. In January 2016 the stock market plummeted. In a matter of days, $2.3 trillion went up in smoke. For investors, it was the worst ten-day start to a year in history. The world was freaking out, convinced that the Big One was finally here! But Ray Dalio, the most successful hedge fund manager of all time, had done something priceless in *Money: Master the Game*: he'd shared with me a unique investment portfolio that could prosper in "all seasons."

In the middle of this market nosedive, Ray was in Davos, Switzerland, where the global elite gather each year to discuss the state of the world. He went on TV, appearing against the backdrop of a snow-covered mountain, to explain how people could protect themselves from this terrifying turmoil. His advice? They should pick up a copy of my book, *Money: Master The*

Game. "Tony Robbins did the layman's version of this all-weather portfolio," he explained. "That might be helpful for people."

So what would have happened if you'd followed Ray's advice and built the all-weather portfolio described in my book? While the Standard & Poor's (S&P) 500 stock index (a list of the top five hundred companies in the United States) dropped 10% in the first few days of 2016, you would have actually made a small *profit* (just under 1%). This portfolio is not meant to be one-size-fits-all, nor is it intended to be the greatest performer. It's meant to provide a smoother ride for those unable to stomach the volatility of a portfolio with a higher percentage of stocks (which can also lead to higher returns).

But what's really amazing is that this portfolio for all seasons would have made money 85% of the time over the last 75 years. That's the power of having the right strategy—a strategy that comes directly from one of the best in the world.

AVOID THE SHARKS

My third reason for writing this book is that I want to show you how to avoid getting eaten by sharks. As we'll discuss later, one of the biggest obstacles to achieving financial success is the difficulty of figuring out who you *can* and *cannot* trust.

There are plenty of fantastic human beings working in the financial field—people who always remember their mom's birthday, who are kind to dogs, and who have impeccable personal hygiene. But they're not necessarily looking out for *your* best interests. Most people who you think are providing unbiased financial "advice" are actually brokers, even if they prefer to go by other titles. They make hefty commissions by selling products, whether it's stocks, bonds, mutual funds, retirement accounts, insurance, or whatever else might pay for their next trip to the Bahamas. As you'll soon learn, only a tiny subset of advisors is *legally required* to put your best interests ahead of its own.

After writing *Money: Master the Game*, I saw once again how easy it is to get fooled by Wall Street. Peter Mallouk, a certified financial planner and attorney whom I respect tremendously, arranged a meeting with me to share what he cryptically described as "some crucial information." **The investment magazine *Barron's* rated Peter and his company, Creative Planning, the number one independent financial advisor in America in 2013, 2014, 2015, and again in 2017 (as the top wealth management firm). *Forbes* named it the top investment advisor in the United States in 2016 (based on 10-year growth), and CNBC ranked it as the number one US wealth management firm in 2014 and 2015**. When someone with Peter's expertise and reputation reaches out to me, I know that I'll learn something of real value.

Peter flew specially from his home in Kansas to meet me in Los Angeles, where I was conducting an Unleash the Power Within event. It was there that he dropped the bomb, explaining how some financial "advisors" who market themselves as straight shooters were actually exploiting a grey area in the law to sell products that benefited themselves. They claimed to be fiduciaries: a small minority of advisors who are legally obligated to put their clients' interests first. In reality, they were unscrupulous salespeople who profited by misrepresenting themselves. *Unshakeable* will give you all the information you need to protect yourself from wolves in sheep's clothing. Equally important, we'll give you the tools and criteria to help you identify honest, conflict-free advisors who will *truly* look out for your best interests.

That meeting formed the basis of a close friendship with Peter and led to his becoming the coauthor of this book. You couldn't ask for a more knowledgeable, honest, or straight-talking guide for this journey. He tells it like it is, and he knows where the bodies are buried!

Peter's firm, which manages $35 billion in assets, is unique. Many billionaires have what's called a "family office": an in-house team that provides them with sophisticated advice on everything from investing and insurance to tax preparation and estate planning. Peter offers this same level of comprehensive advice to clients with assets of $500,000 or more: doctors, dentists, lawyers, small business owners. They're the heartbeat of the American economy, and he believes they deserve no less care and attention than the ultrarich.

I was so impressed with Peter's vision in creating a "family office for all" that I became chief of investor psychology, and engaged the firm to manage my investments and financial planning. I then approached Peter with a radical idea: Would he be willing to create a division that provides the same type of comprehensive service to clients who are early in their wealth-building journey—those with as little as $100,000 in total assets? Peter, who shares my commitment to helping as many people as possible, has done exactly that.

I'm happy to tell you that if you have $100,000 or more in investable assets, his company will provide a complimentary review of your current portfolio and give you specific feedback as it relates to your goals. You may decide that you'd prefer to handle your finances alone. But if you ever decide that it might be helpful to get a second opinion from the top-ranked firm in the country, you're welcome to reach out to Creative Planning, at **www.getasecondopinion.com**.

THE ROAD AHEAD

Before we go any further, I want to quickly show you a map of the road ahead, so you can see for yourself how the chapters that follow will help you. *Unshakeable* is divided into three sections. The first is your Rule Book for Wealth & Financial Success. Why start with a rule book? *Because if you don't know the rules of the game, how can you expect to win?*

What holds many of us back is a feeling that we're in over our heads. It doesn't help that the financial world seems overwhelmingly complex. There are more than 40,000 stocks to choose from in the world today, including 3,700 on various US stock exchanges. By the end of 2015, there were more than 9,500 mutual funds in America alone, which means there are far more funds here than stocks! How ridiculous is that? Add to that nearly 1,600 exchange-traded funds, and you're faced with so many different investment choices that your head starts to spin. Can you imagine standing at an ice-cream counter and having to choose from 50,000 flavors?

You and I need some robust rules so that we can bring order to this chaos. As you'll discover in chapter 3, one of the simplest yet most important rules is this: fees matter.

The vast majority of mutual funds are actively managed, which means they're run by people who attempt to pick the best investments at the best time. Their goal is to "beat the market." For example, they'll attempt to outperform an unmanaged basket of leading stocks such as the S&P 500 index, which is just one of many different indexes that track specific markets throughout the world. But the difference is, actively managed mutual fund companies charge fat fees in return for this service. Sounds fair enough, right?

The problem is, most funds do a terrific job of charging high fees but a terrible job of picking successful investments. One study showed that 96% of mutual funds failed to beat the market over a 15-year period.[1] **The result? You overpay for underperformance.** It's like paying for a Ferrari and then driving home from the dealership in a beaten-up tractor splattered with mud.

HEDGE FUNDS VS. MUTUAL FUNDS VS. INDEX FUNDS

For those unfamiliar, a hedge fund is a private fund available only to high-net-worth investors. The managers have complete flexibility to bet on both directions of the market (up or down). They charge hefty management fees (typically 2%) and share in the profits (typically 20% of profits go to the manager). A mutual fund is a public fund available to anyone. In most cases, they are actively managed by a team who assembles a portfolio of stocks, bonds, or other assets and continually trades their holdings in hopes to beat the "market." An index fund is also a public fund but requires no "active" managers. The fund simply owns all the stocks in the index (for example, they would own all 500 stocks in the S&P 500 index).

Even worse, those fees add up massively over time. **If you overpay by 1% a year, it will cost you 10 years' worth of retirement income.**[2] Once we've shown you how to avoid funds that overcharge and underperform, you could easily save yourself as much as 20 years of income.

1 Industry expert Robert Arnott, founder of Research Affiliates, studied the performance over 15 years of all 203 actively managed mutual funds that had at least $100 million under management.

2 This assumes two investors with a starting investment of $100,000, equal returns of 8% over 30 years, but with 1% fees and 2% fees, respectively. Assuming an equal withdrawal amount at retirement, the investor paying 2% in fees will run out of money 10 years sooner.

If that's all you learn from the first section of this book, it will transform your future. But there's much more. As we mentioned earlier, we'll also show you how to avoid salespeople who provide self-serving "advice" that's hazardous to your financial health, and how to find sophisticated advisors who aren't conflicted. As the saying goes, "When a person with experience meets a person with money, the person with experience ends up with the money; and the person with money ends up with an experience." **We'll show you how to navigate this game so you'll never get taken again.**

The second section of *Unshakeable* is a financial playbook. It will show you exactly what to do so you can put your action plan in place *right now*. Most important, you'll learn the "Core Four": a set of simple yet powerful principles that are derived from my interviews with more than 50 of the world's greatest investors. Though they have many different ways of making money, I've observed that they all share these fundamental decision-making principles. I've found the Core Four transformational in my own financial life, and I'm excited to make this knowledge available to you, too.

Next, you'll learn to "slay the bear": in other words, to build a diversified portfolio so that your nest egg won't be destroyed when a bear market finally comes. *In fact, you'll learn to profit massively from the opportunities that fear and turmoil create.* What most people don't realize is that investment success is largely a matter of smart "asset allocation"—of knowing precisely how much of your money to put in different asset classes such as stocks, bonds, real estate, gold, and cash. The great news is that you'll learn to do this from money masters like Ray Dalio, David Swensen, and our very own Peter Mallouk.

If you already know a bit about investing, you may be wondering—as one financial journalist asked me recently—"Isn't it just a simple matter of buying and holding index funds?" Well, Dalio, Swensen, Warren Buffett, and Jack Bogle all told me that indexing is the smartest strategy for regular people like you and me.[3] One reason why is that index funds are designed

---

3 According to the financial website Investopedia: "Active managers rely on analytical research, forecasts, and their own judgment and experience in making investment decisions on what securities to buy, hold, and sell. The opposite of active management is called passive management, better known as 'indexing.'"

to match the returns of the market. Unless you're a superstar like Warren or Ray, you're better off capturing that market return instead of trying—and almost certainly failing—to beat the market. Even better, index funds charge minuscule fees, saving you a fortune over the long run.

I wish it were that simple, though. As a lifelong student of human behavior, I can tell you this: most people find it really hard to sit tight and stay in the market when everything is going haywire. Buy and hold tends to go out the window. If you have nerves of steel like Buffett or Bogle, that's great. But if you want to know how the majority of people behave under stress, just check out a study by Dalbar, one of the financial industry's leading research firms.

Dalbar revealed the gigantic discrepancy between the *market's* returns and the returns that people *actually* achieve. For instance, the S&P 500 returned an average of 10.28% a year from 1985 to 2015. At this rate, your money doubles every seven years. Thanks to the power of compounding, you'd have made a killing just by owning an index fund that tracked the S&P 500 over those 30 years. Let's say you'd invested $50,000 in 1985. How much would it have been worth by 2015? The answer: $941,613.61. That's right. Almost a million bucks!

But while the market returned 10.28% per year, Dalbar found that the average investor made only 3.66% a year over those three decades! At that rate, your money doubles only every 20 years. The result? Instead of that million-dollar windfall, you ended up with only $146,996.

What explains this massive performance gap? In part, it's the disastrous effect of excessive management fees, outrageous brokerage commissions, and other hidden costs that we'll discuss in chapter 3. These expenses are a constant drain on your returns—the equivalent of a merciless vampire sucking your blood each night while you're asleep.

But there's another culprit, too: human nature. As you and I know, we're emotional creatures with a gift for doing crazy stuff under the influence of emotions such as fear and greed. As the legendary Princeton University economist Burton Malkiel told me: "Emotions get ahold of us, and we, as investors, tend to do very stupid things." For example, "we tend to put money into the market and take it out at exactly the wrong time." You probably know people who got carried away during a bull market and took reckless risks with money they couldn't afford to lose. You may also know people who got scared and sold all their stocks in 2008, only to miss out on huge gains when the market rebounded in 2009.

I've spent almost four decades teaching the psychology of wealth. So, in the third section of *Unshakeable*, I'll show you how to adjust your behavior and avoid common mistakes that are driven by emotion. Why is this so important? Because you can't apply the winning strategies in this book unless you learn to "silence the enemy within."

Then, together we'll answer what may be the most important questions of all. What are you *really* after? How do you achieve the ultimate level of happiness you desire in your life? **Is it really *money* you're chasing, or is it the *feelings* that you think money can create?** Many of us believe—or fantasize—that money will bring us to a point where we finally feel free, secure, excited, empowered, alive, and joyful. But the truth is, you can achieve that beautiful state *right now*, regardless of your level of material wealth. So why wait to be happy?

Finally, in the appendix, we've included an invaluable road map to use with your financial advisors and attorney. These four checklists will guide you in protecting your assets, building your financial legacy, and insuring against the unknown. Plus, you'll discover even more ways to save on taxes!

THE SNAKE AND THE ROPE

But first I want to tell you about the very next chapter, because I'm convinced that it will change your financial life. In fact, even if you read *only* chapter 2 and ignore everything else in this book, you're getting on track to reap amazing rewards!

As I mentioned earlier, this is a time of tremendous uncertainty for most people. The global economy is still limping along after all these years. Middle-class salaries have stagnated for decades. Technology is disrupting so many industries that we don't even know what jobs will exist in the future. And then there's that nagging feeling that a bear market is overdue after years of strong returns. I don't know about you, but all this uncertainty is making many people fearful—and this prevents them from building wealth by investing in the financial markets and becoming long-term owners of this economy, not just consumers.

The next chapter is the antidote to that fear. We'll walk you through seven specific facts that will transform your understanding of how the market works, and of the economic and emotional patterns driving it. You'll learn that corrections and crashes occur with surprising regularity but *never* last. The best investors prepare for this volatility—these dramatic ups and downs—and turn it to their advantage. **Once you understand these patterns, you can act without fear, not because you're in denial but because you have the knowledge and clarity of mind to make the right decisions**.

The stock market has fewer ups-and-downs than my romantic relationships.

This reminds me of an old story you may remember about a Buddhist monk traveling home one night on a rural path. He catches sight of a poisonous snake blocking his way, panics, and runs for dear life in the opposite direction. The next morning, he returns to this scene of terror. But now, in the brightness of day, he realizes that the coiled snake in his path was just a harmless piece of rope.

Chapter 2 will show you that your own anxiety is equally unfounded—that the snake you fear is really just a rope. Why does this matter so much? **Because you can't win this game unless you have the emotional fortitude**

to get *in* it and *stay* in it for the long term. Once you realize that there's no snake blocking your way, you can walk calmly and confidently on the path to financial freedom.

Are you ready? Then let's begin!

THE MOBILE APP AND PODCAST

There are a couple of additional resources to accelerate your journey. First, we created a mobile app containing videos, planning tools, and a personalized calculator that will help you discover how much you need to accumulate in order to achieve different levels of financial security and freedom. Second is the *Unshakeable* podcast. Peter Mallouk and I recorded a series of brief conversations around the core principles of becoming Unshakeable.

Visit **www.Unshakeable.com** for these and other tools, tips, and resources.

CHAPTER 2

WINTER IS COMING . . . BUT WHEN?

These Seven Facts Will Free You from the Fear of Corrections and Crashes

The key to making money in equities is not to get scared out of them.
—PETER LYNCH, who returned 29% a year as a
famed fund manager at Fidelity Investments

Power. The ability to shape and influence life's circumstances. The fuel to produce extraordinary results. Where does it comes from? What makes a person powerful? What creates power in your own life?

When humans lived as hunter-gatherers, we had no power. We were at the mercy of nature. We could be ripped apart by vicious predators or destroyed by brutal weather whenever we ventured into the wild to hunt or scavenge for food. And food wasn't always there. **But gradually, over many thousands of years, we developed an invaluable skill: we learned to recognize—and *utilize*—patterns.**

Most important, we observed the patterns of the seasons. And we learned to take advantage of them by planting crops at the *right* time. This capability moved us from scarcity to abundance—to a way of life in which communities and eventually cities and civilizations could flourish. Our gift for pattern recognition literally changed the course of human history.

Along the way, we also learned a vitally important lesson: we're *not* rewarded when we do the right thing at the wrong time. If you plant in winter, you'll get nothing but pain, no matter how hard you work. To survive and thrive, you and I have to do the right thing at the right time.

Our capacity for pattern recognition is also the number one skill

**that can empower us to achieve financial prosperity. Once you rec-
ognize the patterns in the financial markets, you can adapt to them,
utilize them, and profit from them.** This chapter will give you that power.

> The majority of investors fail to take full advantage of the incredible
> power of compounding—the multiplying power of growth times growth.
> —BURTON MALKIEL

Before we get to the heart of this chapter, let's just take two minutes to discuss a fundamental concept that I'm sure you already know, but one that we
need to utilize and maximize in order to build lasting wealth.

The first pattern we need to recognize is that there's a miraculously powerful way to build wealth that's available to all of us—one that Warren Buffett
has harnessed to amass a fortune that now stands at $65 billion. **What's his
secret? It's simple, says Buffett: "My wealth has come from a combination of living in America, some lucky genes, and compound interest."**

I can't vouch for your genes, though I'm guessing they're pretty good!
What I *do* know for sure is that compounding is a force that can catapult you
to a life of total financial freedom. Of course, we all know about compounding, but it's worth reminding ourselves just how impactful it can be when we
truly understand how to make it work for us. In fact, our ability to recognize
and utilize the power of compounding is the life-changing equivalent of our
ancestors' discovery that they could produce bountiful harvests by planting
crops at the right time!

Let's illustrate the tremendous impact of compounding with just one simple but mind-blowing example. Two friends, Joe and Bob, decide to invest
$300 a month. Joe gets started at age 19, keeps going for eight years, and
then stops adding to this pot at age 27. In all, he's saved a total of $28,800.

Joe's money then compounds at a rate of 10% a year (which is roughly the
historic return of the US stock market over the last century). **By the time
he retires at 65, how much does he have? The answer: $1,863,287. In
other words, that modest investment of $28,800 has grown to nearly
two million bucks! Pretty stunning, huh?**

His friend Bob gets off to a slower start. He begins investing exactly the
same amount—$300 a month—but doesn't get started until age 27. Still, he's

a disciplined guy, and he keeps investing $300 every month until he's 65—a period of 39 years. His money also compounds at 10% a year. The result? When he retires at 65, he's sitting on a nest egg of $1,589,733.

Let's think about this for a moment. Bob invested a total of $140,000, almost five times more than the $28,800 that Joe invested. Yet Joe has ended up with an extra $273,554. That's right: Joe ends up richer than Bob, despite the fact that he never invested a dime after the age of 27!

What explains Joe's incredible success? Simple. *By starting earlier, the compound interest he earns on his investment adds more value to his account than he could ever add on his own.* By the time he reaches age 53, the compound interest on his account adds over $60,000 per year to his balance. By the time he's 60, his account is growing by more than $100,000 per year! All without adding another dime. Bob's total return on the money he invested is 1,032%, whereas Joe's return is a spectacular 6,370%.

Now let's imagine for a moment that Joe *didn't* stop investing at age 27. Instead, like Bob, he kept adding $300 a month until he was 65. The result: he ends up with a nest egg of $3,453,020! In other words, he has $1.86 million more than Bob because he started investing 8 years earlier.

That's the awesome power of compounding. Over time this force can turn a modest sum of money into a *massive* fortune.

But you know what's amazing? Most people never take full advantage of this secret that's lying in full view, this wealth-building miracle that's sitting there right in front of their eyes. Instead, they continue to believe that they can *earn* their way to riches. It's a common misperception—this belief that, if your earned income is big enough, you'll become financially free.

The truth is, it's not that simple. We've all read stories about movie stars, musicians, and athletes who earned more money than God yet ended up broke because they didn't know how to *invest* that income. After a series of lousy investments, the rapper 50 Cent recently declared bankruptcy—despite having had a net worth estimated at $155 million. Actress Kim Basinger, at the height of her popularity, was pulling in more than $10 million per film. And yet she also ended up bankrupt. Even the King of Pop, Michael Jackson, who reportedly signed a recording contract worth almost $1 billion and sold more than 750 million records, supposedly owed more than $300 million upon his death in 2009.

Amount Invested:
3,600
Rate of Return:
10%

$300/monthly ($3,600 annually) growing at 10%				
Age	Joe	Amount	Bob	Amount
19	3,600	3,960	-	-
20	3,600	8,316	-	-
21	3,600	13,108	-	-
22	3,600	18,378	-	-
23	3,600	24,176	-	-
24	3,600	30,554	-	-
25	3,600	37,569	-	-
26	3,600	45,286	-	-
27	-	49,815	3,600	3,960
28	-	54,796	3,600	8,316
29	-	60,276	3,600	13,108
30	-	66,303	3,600	18,378
31	-	72,934	3,600	24,176
32	-	80,227	3,600	30,554
33	-	88,250	3,600	37,569
34	-	97,075	3,600	45,286
35	-	106,782	3,600	53,775
36	-	117,461	3,600	63,112
37	-	129,207	3,600	73,383
38	-	142,127	3,600	84,682
39	-	156,340	3,600	97,110
40	-	171,974	3,600	110,781
41	-	189,171	3,600	125,819
42	-	208,088	3,600	142,361
43	-	228,897	3,600	160,557
44	-	251,787	3,600	180,573
45	-	276,966	3,600	202,590
46	-	304,662	3,600	226,809
47	-	335,129	3,600	253,450
48	-	368,641	3,600	282,755
49	-	405,506	3,600	314,990
50	-	446,056	3,600	350,449
51	-	490,662	3,600	389,454
52	-	539,728	3,600	432,360
53	-	593,701	3,600	479,556
54	-	653,071	3,600	531,471
55	-	718,378	3,600	588,578
56	-	790,216	3,600	651,396
57	-	869,237	3,600	720,496
58	-	956,161	3,600	796,506
59	-	1,051,777	3,600	880,116
60	-	1,156,955	3,600	972,088
61	-	1,272,650	3,600	1,073,256
62	-	1,399,915	3,600	1,184,542
63	-	1,539,907	3,600	1,306,956
64	-	1,693,897	3,600	1,441,612
65	-	**$1,863,287**	3,600	1,589,733
Advantage of investing early:		**$273,554**		

Or more recently, Johnny Depp—one of the highest paid actors in Hollywood, who made more than $650 million in the last 30 years on blockbusters like *Pirates of the Caribbean* and as the face of luxury brands like Dior— is now reported to be in serious financial trouble. While he maintains it's due to his financial managers mismanagement, his managers point to his lavish spending. Depp, according to his managers, was spending $30,000 per month on wine, and even paid $3 million to blast the ashes of Hunter S. Thompson out of a custom-made cannon. You can't make this stuff up!

The lesson? You're never going to *earn* your way to financial freedom. The real route to riches is to set aside a portion of your money and invest it, so that it compounds over many years. That's how you become wealthy while you sleep. That's how you make money your slave instead of being a slave to money. That's how you achieve true financial freedom.

By now, you're probably thinking to yourself, "Yeah, but how much money do I have to set aside in order to reach my financial goals?" That's a great question! As mentioned, to help you answer it, we've developed a mobile app that you can use to figure out exactly what you'll need to save and invest. It's available at www.unshakeable.com.

Everyone's situation is unique, so I'd recommend sitting down with a financial advisor to discuss your specific goals and how to reach them. But I want to warn you, most advisors grossly underestimate how much money you're likely to need to be financially secure, independent, or free. Some say you should have a nest egg that's ten times what you earn currently. Others, who are a bit more realistic, say you'll need fifteen times. In other words, if you're making $100,000, you'll need $1.5 million. If you're making $200,000, you'll need $3 million. You get the idea.

In reality, the number you should *really* aim for is *20* times your income. So, if you currently earn $100,000, you'll need $2 million. It may sound like a lot, but remember that our friend Joe got there with a mere $28,000, and my bet is you'll have much more than this to invest over the coming years.

You can read about this in greater detail in *Money: Master the Game*, which has an entire section on this subject. As I explain there, it's easy to get overwhelmed when you look at a huge number like this. But it's less intimidating when you start with an easier target. For example, maybe your first goal is financial security—not total independence. **How would you feel if you** could cover the cost of your mortgage, food, utilities, transportation, and insurance, all without ever working again? Pretty great, right? The good news is, this number is usually 40% less than ultimate financial independence, where everything you need is paid for, and thus you can hit it quicker. Once you hit *that* target, you'll have built up so much momentum that the bigger number won't feel like such a stretch.

But how are you going to get there? First, you've got to save and invest—become an owner, not just a consumer. Pay yourself first by taking a percentage of your income and having it deducted automatically from your paycheck or bank account. **This will build your Freedom Fund: the source of life-time income that will allow you to never have to work again.** My guess is you're already doing this. But maybe it's time to give yourself a raise: increase what you save from 10% of your income to 15%, or from 15% to 20%.

For some people, 10% may seem impossible right now. Maybe you're at a stage in your life when you have student loans or major obligations to your family or a business. No matter what your situation, you have to take the first step and get underway. There's a proven method called "Save More Tomorrow," which I describe in detail in Chapter 1.3 of *Money: Master the Game*. You start by saving just 3% and gradually raise this to 15% or 20% over time.

Now that you've saved it, where are you going to invest for the maximum returns so that you reach your target faster?

The single best place to compound money over many years is in the stock market. In chapter 6, we'll discuss the importance of putting together a diversified portfolio that includes other assets. But for now, we're going to focus on the stock market. Why? Because this is incredibly fertile land! Like our ancestors, we need to plant our seeds where we can reap the greatest harvest.

WHERE SHOULD I PUT MY MONEY?

As you and I both know, the stock market has made millions of people rich. Over the last 200 years, despite many ups and downs, it's been *the* best place for the long-term investor to build wealth.[4] But you need to understand

---

4 For more information, see the chart on page 309 of *Money: Master the Game* from Nobel Prize–winning economist Robert Schiller.

the market's patterns. You need to understand its seasons. That's what this chapter is all about.

What's the biggest financial question on all of our minds today? In my experience, we're all searching for answers to pretty much the same question: **"Where should I put my money?"**

This question has become more urgent lately because all of the answers seem unappealing. In an era of compressed interest rates, you earn *nothing* when you keep your cash in a savings account. If you buy a high-quality bond (for example, if you lend money to the Swiss or Japanese governments), you'll earn *less* than nothing! There's a joke going around that traditionally safe investments like these now offer "return-free risks" instead of "risk-free returns!"

What about stocks? Hundreds of billions of dollars from all over the globe have poured into the US stock market, which many people regard as a relatively safe haven in an uncertain world. But that's created even greater uncertainty because US stock prices—and valuations—have soared over the past seven and a half years, fueling fears that the market is bound to plunge. Even people who've done well in this rising market are worried that the whole thing could fold, that there's nothing propping it up except the central banks and their crazy policies!

So what should you do? Prepare for a stock market meltdown by selling everything and running to the hills? Keep all of your money in cash (earning zilch) and wait till the market plummets so you can buy in at lower prices? But how long can you wait? What about all those unfortunate souls who've already waited for years, missing the entire bull market? Or should you stay in the market, sit tight, close your eyes, and assume the "brace position" as you prepare for impact? I told you: none of these options sounds that enticing!

As you know, humans have a tough time handling uncertainty. So how are we supposed to make intelligent decisions in this environment where *everything* seems uncertain? What can we do if we have no idea when the market will plunge—when the financial equivalent of winter will finally arrive?

But I've got news for you: we *do* know when winter will arrive. How? Because when we look back at the stock market over an entire century, we discover this extraordinary fact: financial winter comes, on average, *every* year.

Once you start to recognize long-term patterns like this, you can utilize

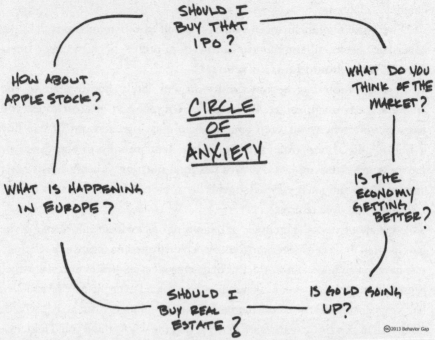

SHOULD I BUY THAT IPO?

HOW ABOUT APPLE STOCK?

WHAT DO YOU THINK OF THE MARKET?

CIRCLE OF ANXIETY

WHAT IS HAPPENING IN EUROPE?

IS THE ECONOMY GETTING BETTER?

SHOULD I BUY REAL ESTATE?

IS GOLD GOING UP?

©2013 Behavior Gap

them. Even better, your fear of uncertainty melts away because you see that important aspects of the financial markets are much more predictable than you'd ever realized.

So, we're going to walk you through seven facts that will show you how the markets work. You'll learn that certain patterns repeat again and again. And you'll learn to base your decisions on an understanding of those proven patterns—just like our ancestors who discovered that planting seeds in spring was a winning strategy. Of course, nothing is ever entirely certain in farming, financial markets, or life! Some winters arrive sooner, some later; some are severe, some mild. But when you stick with an effective approach over many years, your probability of success increases massively. What separates the money masters from the crowd is this ability to find a winning strategy and stick with it, so the odds are always strongly in their favor.

Once you understand the seven indisputable facts we're about to explain, you'll know how the financial seasons work. You'll know the rules of the game—the principles on which it's based. This will give you an enormous edge, since even many experienced and sophisticated investors don't know these facts.

Armed with this knowledge, you can get in the game, stay in it, and win. **Best of all, these facts will free you from all of the fear and anxiety that dominate most people's financial lives. That's why we call them Freedom Facts.**

And let me tell you, the ability to invest without fear is critically important. Why? Because so many people are so paralyzed by fear that they can barely bring themselves to dip their toes in the water. They're terrified that the stock market will crash and wash away all of their hard-earned savings. They're terrified that stocks will nosedive right after they invest. They're terrified that they'll get hurt because they don't know what they're doing. But as you'll soon discover, all those fears will quickly fall away once you understand the pattern of facts that we're going to reveal over the next few pages.

But before we get started, let me quickly explain some investment jargon. **When any market falls by at least 10% from its peak, it's called a correction—a peculiarly bland and neutral term for an experience that most people relish about as much as dental surgery! When a market falls by at least 20% from its peak, it's called a bear market.**

We'll begin by sharing some surprising Freedom Facts about corrections. Then we'll turn our attention to bear markets. **Finally, we'll explain the most important fact of all: the biggest danger isn't a correction or a bear market, it's being *out* of the market.**

Freedom Fact 1: On Average, Corrections Have Occurred About Once a Year Since 1900

Have you ever listened to the pundits on CNBC or MSNBC talking about the stock market? Isn't it amazing how dramatic they can make it sound? They love talking about volatility and turmoil because fear draws you into their programming. They're constantly analyzing minicrises that prognosticators predict could trigger market mayhem. The crisis in question might be unrest in the Middle East, slumping oil prices, the downgrading of US debt, a "fiscal cliff," a budget standoff, Brexit, a China slowdown, or whatever else they can milk for excitement. And by the way, if you don't understand these things, don't worry: most of these experts don't either!

I don't blame them for peddling drama. It's their job. But between you and me, none of this is *really* that exciting. A lot of it is just hyped up to stop you from reaching for your remote control. The trouble is, all this babble, all this drama, all this emotion can make it hard for us to think clearly. When we hear these "experts" speaking in grave voices about the possibility of a correction or a crash or a crisis, it's easy to become anxious because it sounds like the sky is about to fall. It might make for good TV, but the last thing you and I want is to make fear-based financial decisions. So we have to remove as much emotion as possible from this game.

Instead of getting distracted by all this noise, it helps to focus on a few key facts that truly matter. **For example, on average, *there's been a market correction every year since 1900.*** When I first heard this, I was floored. **Just think about it: if you're 50 years old today and have a life expectancy of 85, you can expect to live through another 35 corrections. To put it another way, you'll experience the same number of corrections as birthdays!**

Why does this matter? Because it shows you that corrections are just a routine part of the game. Instead of living in fear of them, you and I have to accept them as regular occurrences—like spring, summer, fall, and winter. And you know what else? **Historically, the average correction has lasted *only 54 days*—less than two months!** In other words, most corrections are over almost before you know it. Not that scary, right?

Still, when you're in the midst of a correction, you might find yourself becoming emotional and wanting to sell because you're anxious to avert the possibility of more pain. You're certainly not alone. These widespread emotions create a crisis mentality. **But it's important to note that, in the average correction over the last 100 years, the market has fallen only 13.5%. From 1980 through the end of 2015, the average drop was 14.2%.**

It can feel pretty uncomfortable when your assets are taking that kind of a hit—and the uncertainty leads many people to make big mistakes. But here's what you have to remember: if you hold tight, it's highly likely that the storm will soon pass.

*Freedom Fact 2: Less Than 20% of All
Corrections Turn Into a Bear Market*

When the market starts tumbling—especially when it's down more than 10%—many people hit their pain threshold and start to sell because they're scared that this drop could turn into a death spiral. Aren't they just being sensible and prudent? Actually, not so much. **It turns out that *fewer than one in five corrections escalate to the point where they become a bear market.* To put it another way, 80% of corrections *don't* turn into bear markets.**

If you panic and move into cash during a correction, you may well be doing so right before the market rebounds. Once you understand that the vast majority of corrections aren't that bad, it's easier to keep calm and resist the temptation to hit the eject button at the first sign of turbulence.

Freedom Fact 3: Nobody Can Predict Consistently Whether the Market Will Rise or Fall

The media perpetuates a myth that, if you're smart enough, you can predict the market's moves and avoid its downdrafts. The financial industry sells the same fantasy: economists and "market strategists" from big investment banks confidently predict where the S&P 500 will stand at the end of the year, as if they have a crystal ball or (equally unlikely) superior insight.

Newsletter writers also love to act like Nostradamus and warn you of the "coming crash," hoping you'll feel compelled to subscribe to their services so you can avoid this fate. Many of them make the same dire predictions every year until they're occasionally right, as anyone would be. After all, even a man with a broken watch can tell you the correct time twice a day. These self-proclaimed seers then use that "accurate" prediction to market themselves as the next great market timer. Unless you're wise to this trick, it's easy to fall for it.

Some of these folks may actually believe in their own powers of prediction; others are just slick salesmen. So take your pick: Are they idiots or liars? I couldn't possibly say! But I'll tell you this: if you're ever tempted to take them seriously, just remind yourself of this classic remark from the physicist Niels Bohr: "Prediction is very difficult, especially about the future."

I'm not sure how you feel about the tooth fairy or the Easter Bunny. But when it comes to our finances, it's best to face facts. And the fact is, *nobody* can consistently predict whether markets will rise or fall. It's delusional to think that you or I could successfully "time the market" by jumping in and out at the right moments.

If you're not convinced, here's what two of the wisest masters of the financial world think of market timing and the challenge of predicting market movements. Jack Bogle, the founder of Vanguard, which has more than $3 trillion in assets under management, has said, "Sure, it would be great to get out of the stock market at the high and back in at the low, but in 65 years in the business, I not only have never met anybody that knew how to do it, I've never met anybody who had met anybody that knew how to do it." **And Warren Buffett has said, "The only value of stock forecasters is to make fortune-tellers look good."**

Still, I have to confess, it's fun to watch all these market pundits, commentators, and economists make fools of themselves by trying to pinpoint a correction. Look at the chart on the following page, and you'll see what I mean. One of my favorite examples is economist Dr. Nouriel Roubini, who predicted (wrongly) that there'd be a "significant" stock market correction in 2013. Roubini, one of the best-known forecasters of our time, was nicknamed "Dr. Doom" because of his many prophecies of disaster. He successfully predicted the 2008 market meltdown. Unfortunately, he also warned of a recession in 2004 (wrongly), 2005 (wrongly), 2006 (wrongly), and 2007 (wrongly).

In my experience, market seers like Roubini are clever and articulate, and their arguments are often compelling. But they thrive by scaring the living daylights out of you—and they've been wrong again and again and again. Sometimes they get it right. But if you listen to all of their scary warnings, you'll end up hiding under your bed, clutching a tin box containing your life savings. And let me tell you a secret: historically, that's not been a winning strategy for long-term financial success.

Merchants of Doom

If you'd like, take a moment and look at these 32 failed predictions by self-appointed market forecasters. Each of the numbers below corresponds to the date of the prediction in the graph. The common pattern is they're all predicting that the market will go down when it's actually going up.

1. "Market Correction Ahead," Bert Dohmen, Dohmen Capital Research Group, March 7, 2012.

2. "Stocks Flirt with Correction," Ben Rooney, CNN Money, June 1, 2012.

3. "10% Market Correction Looms: Dig in or Bail Out?," Matt Krantz, *USA Today*, June 5, 2012.

4. "A significant equity-price correction could, in fact, be the force that in 2013 tips the US economy into outright contraction," Nouriel Roubini, Roubini Global Economics, July 20, 2012.

5. "Prepare for Stock Market Crash 2013," Jonathan Yates, moneymorning .com, June 23, 2012.

6. "Dr. Doom 2013 Prediction: Roubini Says Worse Global Economic Turmoil Approaching; Five Factors to Blame," Kukil Bora, *International Business Times*, July 24, 2012.

7. "Watch out for a Correction—or Worse," Mark Hulbert, MarketWatch, August 8, 2012.

8. "It's Coming: One Pro Sees Big Stock Selloff in 10 Days," John Melloy, CNBC, September 4, 2012.

9. "Warning: Stock Correction May Be Coming," Hibah Yousuf, CNN Money, October 4, 2012.

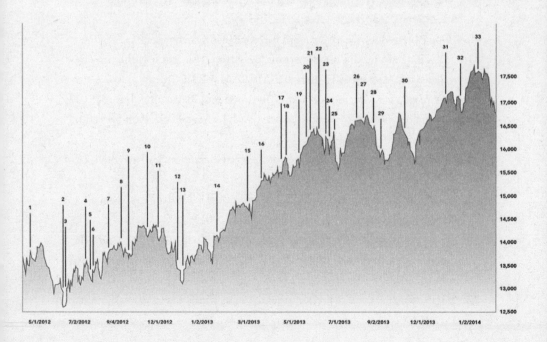

10. "I'm going around town telling my hedge fund clients that the US economy is headed into recession," Michael Belkin, Belkin Limited, October 15, 2012.

11. "Fiscal Cliff Blues May Lead to Correction," Caroline Valetkevitch and Ryan Vlastelica, Reuters, November 9, 2012.

12. "Why a Severe Stock Market Correction's Imminent," Mitchell Clark, Lombardi Financial, November 14, 2012.

13. "By summer, we get another crash," Harry Dent, Dent Research, January 8, 2013.

14. "A Stock Market Correction May Have Begun," Rick Newman, *U.S. News & World Report*, February 21, 2013.

15. "Sluggish Economy May Signal Correction," Maureen Farrell, CNN Money, February 28, 2013.

16. "I think a correction is coming," Byron Wien, Blackstone, April 4, 2013.

17. "Market's Long Overdue Correction Seems to Be Starting," Jonathan Castle, Paragon Wealth Strategies, April 8, 2013.

18. "5 Warning Signs of a Coming Market Correction," Dawn Bennett, Bennett Group Financial Services, April 16, 2013.

19. "Stock Market Warning Signs Becoming Ominous," Sy Harding, StreetSmartReport.com, April 22, 2013.

20. "Don't buy—sell risk assets," Bill Gross, PIMCO, May 2, 2013.

21. "This may not be the time to sprint away from risk, but it is the time to walk away," Mohamed El-Erian, PIMCO, May 22, 2013.

22. "We're due for a correction soon," Byron Wien, Blackstone, June 3, 2013.

23. "Doomsday poll: 87% Risk of Stock Crash by Year-End," Paul Farrell, MarketWatch, June 5, 2013.

24. "Stock Shrink: Market Heading for Severe Correction," Adam Shell, *USA Today*, June 15, 2013.

25. "Don't Be Complacent—A Market Correction Is On Its Way," Sasha Cekerevac, Investment Contrarians, July 12, 2013.

26. "For Two Months, My Models Have Told Me That July 19th Would Be the Start of a Big Stock Market Sell-Off," Jeff Saut, raymondjames.com, July 18, 2013.

27. "Signs of a Market Correction Ahead," John Kimelman, *Barron's*, August 13, 2013.

28. "Correction Watch: How Soon? How Bad? How to Prepare?," Kevin Cook, Zacks.com, August 23, 2013.
29. "I Think There's a Decent Chance Stocks Will Crash," Henry Blodget, Business Insider, September 26, 2013.
30. "5 Reasons to Expect a Correction," Jeff Reeves, MarketWatch, November 18, 2013.
31. "Time to Brace for a 20% Correction," Richard Rescigno, *Barron's*, December 14, 2013.
32. "Blackstone's Wien: Stock Market Poised for 10% Correction," Dan Weil, Moneynews.com, January 16, 2014.

Freedom Fact 4: The Stock Market Rises over Time
Despite Many Short-Term Setbacks

The S&P 500 index experienced an average intra-year decline of 14.2% from 1980 through the end of 2015. In other words, these market drops were remarkably regular occurrences over 36 years. Once again, nothing to be scared of—just a matter of winter putting in its usual seasonal appearance. But you know what *really* blows my mind? **As you can see in the chart below, the market ended up achieving a positive return in 27 of those 36 years. That's 75% of the time!**

Happy Endings
Despite a 14.2% average drop within each year, the US market ended up with a positive return in 27 of the last 36 years.

Why is this so important? Because it reminds us that the market generally rises over the long run—even though we hit a huge number of potholes along the way. You know as well as I do that the world had its fair share of problems over those 36 years, including two Gulf wars, 9/11, the conflicts in Iraq and Afghanistan, and the worst financial crisis since the Great Depression. Even so, the market ultimately rose in all but 9 of those years.

What does this mean in practical terms? It means that you and I should always remember that the long-term trajectory is likely to be good, even when the short-term news is dismal and the market is getting smacked. We don't need to get bogged down in economic theory here. But it's worth

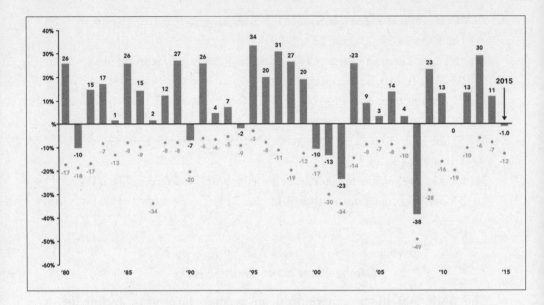

mentioning that the US stock market typically rises over time because the economy expands as American companies become more profitable, as American workers become more efficient and productive, as the population grows, and as technology drives new innovation.

I'm not saying that every company—or every individual stock—will do well over time. As you and I both know, the business world is a Darwinian jungle! Some companies will die, and some stocks will fall to zero. But one big advantage of owning an index fund that tracks a basket of stocks such as the S&P 500 is that the weaker companies intermittently get culled and replaced by stronger ones. It's survival of the fittest in action! The great thing is that you benefit from these upgrades in the quality of the companies in the index. How? Well, as a shareholder of an index fund, you own part of the future cash flows of the companies in that index. This means that the American economy is making you money even while you sleep!

But what if America's economic future is lousy? It's a fair question. We all know there are serious challenges, whether it's the threat of terrorism, global warming, or Social Security liabilities. Even so, this is an incredibly dynamic and resilient economy with some powerful trends driving its future growth. **In his 2015 annual report, Warren Buffett addressed this subject at length, explaining how population growth and extraordinary gains in** productivity will create an enormous increase in wealth for the next generation of Americans. "This all-powerful trend is certain to continue: America's economic magic remains alive and well," he wrote. "For 240 years, it's been a terrible mistake to bet against America, and now is no time to start."

Freedom Fact 5: Historically, Bear Markets Have Happened Every Three to Five Years

I hope you're starting to see why it's a good idea to be a long-term investor in the stock market and not merely a short-term trader. And I hope it's now equally obvious that you don't need to live in fear of corrections. Just to recap for a moment: you know now that corrections happen regularly; that nobody can predict *when* they'll happen; and that the market usually rebounds quickly, resuming its general upward trajectory. Any fear you once felt should turn to power. Believe me, these facts hit me like a revelation: once I understood them, all of my concerns about corrections melted away. **Here was factual proof that the snake was nothing but an inert rope!**

But what about bear markets? Shouldn't we be terrified of *them*? Actually, no. Here again, we need to understand a few key facts so we can act on the basis of knowledge, not emotion.

The first fact you need to know is that there were 34 bear markets in the 115 years between 1900 and 2015. In other words, on average, they happened nearly once every three years. More recently, bear markets have occurred slightly less often: in the 70 years since 1946, there have been 14 of them. **That's a rate of one bear market every five years.** So, depending on when we start counting, it's fair to say that bear markets have historically happened every three to five years. At that rate, if you're 50 years old, you could easily live through another eight or ten bear markets!

You and I both know that the future will *not* be an exact replica of the past. Still, it's useful to study the past to gain a broad sense of these recurring patterns. As the saying goes, "History doesn't repeat itself, but it rhymes." So, what do we learn from more than a century of financial history? We learn that bear markets are likely to continue happening every few years, whether we like it or not. As I said before, winter is coming. So, we'd better get used to it—and prepare.

How bad does it get when the market *really* crashes? Well, historically, the S&P 500 has dropped by an average of 33% during bear markets. **In more than a third of bear markets, the index plunged by more than 40%.** I'm not going to sugarcoat this. If you're someone who panics, sells everything in the midst of this mayhem, and locks in a loss of more than 40%, you're going to feel like a grizzly bear mauled you *for real*. Even if you have the knowledge and fortitude *not* to sell, you'll likely find that bear markets are a gut-wrenching experience.

Even an old warhorse like my buddy Jack Bogle admits that they're no walk in the park. "How do I feel when the market goes down 50%?" he asks rhetorically. "Honestly, I feel miserable. I get knots in my stomach. So what do I do? I get out a couple of my books on 'staying the course' and reread them!"

Sadly, many advisors fall victim to the same fear and hide under their desks during these tumultuous times. Peter Mallouk told me that the on-going communication during these storms is what sets Creative Planning apart. His company is the proverbial lighthouse, broadcasting the message "Stay the course!"

But here's what you need to know: bear markets don't last. If you look at the chart on the next page, you'll see what happened in the 14 bear markets we've experienced in the United States over the last 70 years. **They varied widely in duration, from a month and a half (45 days) to nearly 2 years (694 days). On average, they lasted about a year.**

When you're in the midst of a bear market, you'll notice that most of the people around you become consumed with pessimism. They start to believe that the market will never rise again, that their losses will only deepen, that winter will last forever. But remember: winter *never* lasts! Spring always follows.

The most successful investors take advantage of all that fear and gloom, using these tumultuous periods to invest more money at bargain prices. Sir John Templeton, one of the greatest investors of the last century, talked to me at length about this in several interviews I did with him before he passed away in 2008. Templeton, who made a fortune buying cheap stocks in

A Look Back at Bear Markets		
Years	Number of Days in Length	% Decline in S&P 500
1946 - 1947	353	-23.2%
1956 - 1957	564	-19.4%
1961 - 1962	195	-27.1%
1966	240	-25.2%
1968 - 1970	543	-35.9%
1973 - 1974	694	-45.1%
1976 - 1978	525	-26.9%
1981 - 1982	472	-24.1%
1987	101	-33.5%
1990	87	-21.2%
1998	45	-19.3%
2000 - 2001	546	-36.8%
2002	200	-32.0%
2007 - 2009	515	-57.6%

the midst of World War II, explained: **"The best opportunities come in times of maximum pessimism."**

Freedom Fact 6: Bear Markets Become Bull Markets, and Pessimism Becomes Optimism

Do you remember how fragile the world seemed in 2008 when banks were collapsing and the stock market was in free fall? When you pictured the future, did it seem dark and dangerous? Or did it seem like the good times were just around the corner and the party was about to begin?

As you can see from the chart on the next page, the market finally hit rock bottom on March 9, 2009. And do you know what happened next? **The S&P 500 index surged by 69.5% over the next 12 months.** That's a spectacular return! One moment, the market was reeling. The next moment, we began one of the greatest bull markets in history! **As I write this in late 2016, the S&P 500 has risen by an astonishing 266% since its low point in March 2009.**

You might think this was a freak occurrence. But as you can see on the

From Bear to Bull	
Bear Market Bottom	Next 12 Months (S&P 500)
June 13, 1949	42.07%
October 22, 1957	31.02%
June 26, 1962	32.66%
May 26, 1970	43.73%
October 3, 1974	37.96%
August 12, 1982	59.40%
December 4, 1987	22.40%
September 21, 2001	33.73%
July 23, 2002	17.94%
March 9, 2009	69.49%

chart above, the pattern of bear markets suddenly giving way to bull markets has repeated itself again and again in America over the last 75 years.

Now can you see why Warren Buffett says he likes to be greedy when others are fearful? He knows how quickly the mood can switch from fear and despondency to exuberant optimism. In fact, when the mood in the market is overwhelmingly bleak, superinvestors such as Buffett tend to view it as a *positive* sign that better times lie ahead.

You see a similar pattern when it comes to consumer confidence, which is a measure of how optimistic or pessimistic consumers feel about the future. During a bear market, commentators often remark that consumer spending has fallen because people are so nervous about the future. It's a vicious cycle: consumers spend less money, so companies *make* less money. And if companies make less, doesn't that mean the stock market won't be able to recover? You might think so. But these periods of consumer pessimism are often the ideal time to invest. Look at the table on the next page and you'll see that an array of bull markets began when consumer confidence was at a low point.

Why? Because the stock market isn't looking at *today*. The market always looks to *tomorrow*. What matters most isn't where the economy

is right now but *where it's headed*. And when everything seems terrible, the pendulum eventually swings in the other direction. In fact, every single bear market in US history has been followed by a bull market, without exception.

This record of incredible resilience has made life relatively easy for long-term investors in the US market. Again and again, bad times have eventually been followed by good times. But what about other countries? Have they seen a similar pattern of bear markets being followed by bull markets?

Broadly speaking, yes. But Japan has had a much tougher experience. Remember the 1980s when Japanese companies seemed poised to rule the world? Japan's stock index, the Nikkei 225, rose sixfold during those years of giddy optimism, hitting a high of 38,957 in 1989. Then the market got blown to bits. By March 2009, the Nikkei had sunk to a low of 7,055. That's an 82% loss over 20 years! In recent years, though, it has staged a strong comeback, recovering to a high of 17,079. Even so, the Japanese market is still way below its peak after nearly three decades.

As we'll discuss later, you can protect yourself against this sort of disaster by building a portfolio that's broadly diversified globally and also among different types of assets.

Who Needs Confidence?	
Consumer Confidence <60%	Next 12 Months (S&P 500)
1974	+37%
1980	+32%
1990	+30%
2008	+60%
2011	+15%

> The stock market is a device for transferring
> money from the impatient to the patient.
> —WARREN BUFFETT

Did you ever listen to the news and hear the announcer mention that the stock market just hit an all-time high? Maybe you got that queasy feeling that we were flying too close to the sun, that gravity was about to do its thing, that the market would inevitably fall back to earth.

As I'm writing these words, the S&P 500 stands just a few points below its all-time high. In recent weeks, it hit new highs on multiple occasions. And, as you know, this bull market is more than seven years old. So, the possibility that we may be due for a fall has probably been on your mind as well as mine. It certainly makes sense not to take carefree risks when stocks have soared for years. If there's one lesson from Japan's experience, it's that we humans have a natural tendency to get carried away and lose sight of danger when stock prices have been surging.

But the fact that a market is close to its all-time high doesn't necessarily mean that there's trouble ahead. As we discussed earlier, the US market has a general upward bias. It rises over the long term because the economy continues to grow. **In fact, the US market hits an all-time high on approximately 5% of all trading days. On average, that's once a month.**[5]

Thanks to inflation, the price of almost *everything* is at an all-time high almost all the time. If you don't believe me, check the price of your Big Mac, your café latte, your candy bar, your Thanksgiving turkey, or your new car. Chances are, they're all priced at an all-time high, too.

Freedom Fact 7: The Greatest Danger Is Being out of the Market

I hope you agree with me by now that it's not possible to jump in and out of the market successfully. It's just too difficult for regular mortals like you and me to predict the market's movements. As Jack Bogle once said, "The idea

[5] Remember: real life is not an absolute average. You tend to have streaks of up days and also down days. But it's good to know the average.

that a bell rings to signal when investors should get into or out of the stock market is simply not credible." Even so, the fact that the market is hovering close to an all-time high might tempt you to play it safe by waiting on the sidelines in cash until stock prices have fallen.

The trouble is, sitting on the sidelines even for short periods of time may be the costliest mistake of all. I know this sounds counter-intuitive, but as you can see in the chart below, it has a devastating impact on your returns when you miss even a few of the market's best trading days.

You miss one hundred percent of the shots you don't take.

—HOCKEY HALL OF FAMER WAYNE GRETZKY

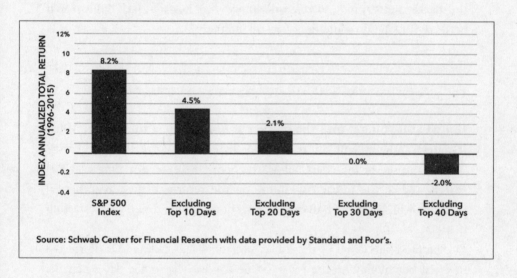

Source: Schwab Center for Financial Research with data provided by Standard and Poor's.

From 1996 through 2015, the S&P 500 returned an average of 8.2% a year. But if you missed out on the top 10 trading days during those 20 years, your returns dwindled to just 4.5% a year. Can you believe it? Your returns would have been cut almost in half just by missing the 10 best trading days in 20 years!

It gets worse! If you missed out on the top 20 trading days, your returns dropped from 8.2% a year to a paltry 2.1%. And if you missed out on the top 30 trading days? Your returns vanished into thin air, falling all the way to zero!

Meanwhile, a study by JPMorgan found that 6 of the 10 *best* days in the market over the last 20 years occurred within two weeks of the 10 *worst* days. The moral: if you got spooked and sold at the wrong time, you missed out on the fabulous days that followed, which is when patient investors made almost *all* of their profits. **In other words, market turmoil isn't something to fear. It's the greatest opportunity for you to leapfrog to financial freedom. You can't win by sitting on the bench. You *have* to be in the game. To put it another way, fear isn't rewarded. Courage is.**

The message is clear: the greatest danger to your financial health isn't a market crash; it's being *out* of the market. In fact, one of the most fundamental rules for achieving long-term financial success is that you need to get *in* the market and *stay* in it, so you can capture all of its gains. Jack Bogle puts it perfectly: "Don't do something—just stand there!"

> Hell is truth seen too late.
>
> —THOMAS HOBBES, seventeenth-century British philosopher

But what if you get into the market at exactly the wrong time? What if you get unlucky, and you're hit immediately by a correction or a crash? As you can see in the chart below, the Schwab Center for Financial Research studied the impact of timing on the returns of five hypothetical investors who had $2,000 in cash to invest once a year for 20 years, starting in 1993.

The most successful of these five investors—let's call her Ms. Perfect—invested her money on the *best* possible day each year: the day when the market hit its exact low point for that year. This mythical investor, who *perfectly* timed the market for 20 years running, ended up with $87,004. The investor with the worst timing—let's call him Mr. Hapless—invested all of his money on the *worst* possible day each year: the day when the market hit its exact high point for that year. The result? He ended up with $72,487.

What's striking is that, even after this 20-year run of spectacularly bad luck, Mr. Hapless *still* made a substantial profit. The lesson? **If you stay in the market long enough, compounding works its magic, and you end up with a healthy return—even if your timing was hopelessly unlucky.** And you know what? **The worst-performing investor wasn't the unlucky**

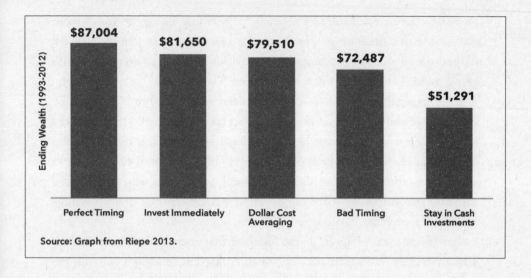

Source: Graph from Riepe 2013.

one, but the one who stayed on the bench, the one in cash: he ended up with only $51,291.

FREE AT LAST!

In this chapter, you've learned seven facts that show you how the market works. Based on more than a century of financial history, you now understand that corrections, bear markets, and recoveries follow similar patterns again and again. Now that you have the power to *recognize* these long-term patterns, you will also have the power to *utilize* them.

Later in this book, we'll explain in depth the specific strategies you can use to take advantage of these seasonal patterns. For example, we'll show you what to look for when creating your ideal asset allocation strategy, so you can minimize your losses in a bear market and maximize your gains when the market rebounds. But for now, you should have a big smile on your face! You know the facts. You know the rules of the game. You know that corrections and bears are to be expected, and you'll soon learn how to take advantage of them. You're one step closer to being truly *unshakeable*.

Best of all, you're taking control of your financial life. You're taking responsibility. Because you know what? Most people never take responsibility. They prefer to blame the market for whatever happens to them. *But the market never took a dime from anyone!* If you lose money in the market, it's because of a decision *you* made—and if you make money in the market, it's because of a decision *you* made. The market is going to do whatever it's going to do. But *you* determine whether you'll win or lose. *You're* in charge.

This chapter has taught you that financial winter is always followed by spring—a lesson that will allow you to proceed without fear. Or, at the very least, a lot less of it. Knowledge brings understanding, and understanding brings resolve. You won't be the person who pulls your money out of stocks when the market is getting slammed! You'll be the one who stays in the game for the long haul—planting the right seeds, nurturing them patiently, and then reaping the harvest!

But in the next chapter, you'll discover that there's one thing that it's actually *healthy* to fear: financial firms that charge clients like you and me outrageous fees for lousy performance. As you'll see, there's no more powerful way to take control of your finances than to cut out these excessive—and often hidden—fees. How will you benefit? You'll save at least 10 years of income! How's that for taking charge?

So turn the page, and let's expose those hidden fees and half-truths . . .

CHAPTER 3

HIDDEN FEES AND HALF-TRUTHS

How Wall Street Fools You into Overpaying for Underperformance

The name of the game? Moving the money from
the client's pocket to your pocket.
—MATTHEW McCONAUGHEY TO LEONARDO
DICAPRIO IN *THE WOLF OF WALL STREET*

I often ask people "What are you investing for?" I get a variety of answers: from "high returns," to "financial security," to "retirement," to "a beach house in Hawaii." But before long, nearly everyone's answers begin to rhyme. **What most people really want, regardless of how much money they have today, is freedom. Freedom to do more of what they want, whenever they want, with whomever they want.** It's a beautiful dream, and an achievable one. But how can you sail off into the sunset if your boat has a hole in it? What if it's slowly but surely taking on so much water that it'll sink long before it reaches its destination?

I hate to tell you this, but most people are in *exactly* this position. They don't realize that they're doomed to disappointment because of the gradual—but ultimately devastating—impact of excessive fees on their financial well-being. What kills me is that they have *no idea* this is even happening to them. They have no idea that they are victims of a financial industry that is surreptitiously but *systematically* overcharging them.

Don't just take my word for it. The nonprofit organization AARP published a report in which it found that 71% of Americans believe that they pay no fees at all to have a 401(k) plan. That's right: 7 out of 10 people are *entirely unaware* that they're even being charged a fee! This is the equivalent of believing that fast food contains no calories. Meanwhile, 92% admit that they have no idea how *much* they're actually paying.[6] In other words, they're blindly trusting the financial industry to look out for their best interests! Yup, that's the very same industry that brought about the global financial crisis! You might as well just hand over your wallet and the password to your debit card.

You know the old saying "Ignorance is bliss"? Well, let me tell you: when it comes to your finances, ignorance is *not* bliss. Ignorance is pain and poverty. Ignorance is disaster for you and your family—and bliss for the financial firms that are exploiting your inattention!

This chapter will shine a bright light on the subject of fees, so you know *exactly* what's going on. The good news: once you know precisely what's happening, you can put a permanent, life-changing stop to it. **Why does this matter so much? Because excessive fees can destroy *two-thirds* of your nest egg!** Jack Bogle spelled it out to me quite simply:

"Let's assume the stock market gives a 7% return over 50 years," he began. At that rate, because of the power of compounding, "each dollar goes up to 30 dollars." But the average fund charges you about 2% per year in costs, which drops your average annual return to 5%. At that rate, "you get 10 dollars. So 10 dollars versus 30 dollars. **You put up 100% of the capital, you took 100% of the risk, and you got 33% of the return!**"

Did you get that? You forfeited two-thirds of *your* nest egg to line the pockets of money managers who took *no* risk, put up *none* of the capital, and often delivered *mediocre* performance! Now who do you think will end up with the beach house in Hawaii?

Once you've read this chapter, you'll know how to take back control! By minimizing fees, you'll save years—or, more likely, *decades*—of retirement income. This one move will dramatically accelerate your journey to financial freedom. But that's not all. You'll also learn how to slash the taxes you pay on your investments. That's crucial because excessive taxes, like fees, are a destructive force that can overwhelm all the positive steps you've taken.

How do you think you'll feel when you've not only identified these two enemies but also defeated them? You'll feel truly unshakeable!

6 "Nine in 10 Americans make this 401(k) mistake: Retirement Scan," http://www .financial-planning.com/news/nine-in-10-americans-make-this-401-k-mistake-retirement -scan.

THE WOLVES OF WALL STREET

If you're looking to achieve financial security, the obvious route is to invest in mutual funds. Maybe your brother-in-law was lucky enough to buy shares in Amazon, Google, and Apple before they skyrocketed. But for the rest of us, picking individual stocks is a losing game. There are just too many things we don't know, too many variables, too much that can go wrong. Mutual funds offer a simple and logical alternative. For a start, they provide you with the benefit of broad diversification, which helps to reduce your overall risk.

But how do you pick the right funds? There are certainly enough to choose from. As we mentioned earlier, there are about 9,500 mutual funds in America—more than *double* the number of publicly traded US companies! So it's safe to say the mutual fund market is a tad saturated. Why do so many companies want to be in this business? Yup, you got it: because it's fabulously lucrative!

The trouble is, it tends to be much more lucrative for Wall Street than for actual customers like you and me. Don't get me wrong. I'm not suggesting that the industry is consciously out to screw us. I'm not suggesting that this is a business full of crooks or charlatans! On the contrary, the majority of financial professionals are intelligent, hardworking, and thoughtful. But Wall Street has evolved into an ecosystem that exists first and foremost to make money for itself. It's not an evil industry made up of evil individuals. It's made up of corporations whose purpose is to maximize profits for their shareholders. That's their job.

Even the best-intentioned employees are working within the confines of this system. They're under intense pressure to grow profits, and they're rewarded for doing so. If you—the client—happen to do well, too, that's great! But don't kid yourself. You're not the priority!

When I met David Swensen, the chief investment officer for Yale University, he helped me to understand just how badly the mutual fund industry serves the majority of its clients. Swensen is the rock star of institutional investing, famous for having turned a $1 billion portfolio into $25.4 billion! But he's also one of the most caring and sincere people I've ever met. He could easily have left Yale and become a billionaire by starting his own hedge fund, but he's guided by a deep sense of duty and service to his alma mater. So I wasn't surprised to hear his dismay at the way many fund companies mistreat their clients.

As he put it: **"Overwhelmingly, mutual funds extract enormous sums from investors in exchange for providing a shocking disservice."**

What service is it that funds are *supposed* to provide? Well, when you buy an actively managed fund, you're essentially paying for the manager to generate market-beating returns. Otherwise wouldn't you be better off just sticking your money in a low-cost index fund, which *attempts to replicate* the returns of the market?

As you can imagine, the people who run actively managed funds are no fools. They aced their math tests in high school, studied economics and accounting, and earned MBAs from the world's best graduate schools. Many of them even wear suits and ties! And they're dedicated to researching and selecting the very best stocks for their funds to own.

So what could possibly go wrong? Pretty much everything . . .

The Human Factor

Fund managers try to add value by predicting which companies will perform best in the weeks, months, or years to come. They can avoid or "underweight" particular sectors (or countries) that they believe have unattractive prospects. They can build up cash if they can't find stocks worth buying—or they can invest more aggressively when they're feeling bullish. **But it turns out that the professionals aren't really any better at predicting the future than the rest of us.** The truth is, humans are generally pretty lousy at making predictions! Perhaps that's why you never see a newspaper headline that says "Psychic Wins the Lottery!"

When active fund managers trade in and out of stocks, there are plenty of opportunities to make mistakes. For example, they don't just have to decide *which* stocks to buy or sell, but *when* to buy or sell them. And every decision obliges them to make another decision. The more decisions they face, the more chances they have to mess up.

To make matters worse, all this trading gets expensive. Every time a fund trades in or out of a stock, a brokerage firm charges a commission to execute the transaction. It's a bit like gambling at a casino: the house gets paid no matter what. So the house *always* wins in the end! In this case, the house is a brokerage firm (like the Swiss financial company UBS or Merrill Lynch, the wealth management division of Bank of America) that charges a toll every time the fund manager makes a move. Over time those tolls add up.

Like poker, investing is a zero-sum game: there are only so many chips on the table. When two people trade a stock, one must win and one must lose. If the stock goes up after you buy it, you win. But you've got to win by a big enough margin to cover those transaction costs.

Wait, it gets worse! If your stock goes up, you'll also have to pay taxes on your profits when you sell the stock. For investors in an actively managed fund, this combination of hefty transaction costs *and* taxes is a silent killer, quietly eating away at the fund's returns! To add value *after* taxes and fees, the fund manager has to win by a *really* big margin. And, as you'll soon see, that ain't easy.

Do your eyes glaze over when we start talking about taxes? I know, I know! This isn't the sexiest topic. But it *should* be! **Because the largest expense in your life is taxes, and paying more than you need to pay is insane—especially when it's absolutely avoidable!** If you're not careful, taxes can have a catastrophic impact on your returns. Here's an extreme yet surprisingly common example:

Let's say you invest in a fund in December. Then, the next day, the manager sells a stock that's shot up over the past 10 months. Since you're now an owner of the fund, you'll be getting a tax bill for those gains, even though *you* didn't benefit one bit from the stock's meteoric rise![7] Nobody said the tax code was fair.

Another common problem has to do with how long actively managed funds hold their investments. Most are trading constantly. They sell many of their investments in less than a year. That means you no longer

---

7 It's called capital gains tax, and you get hit by it even though you didn't earn those capital gains. Owning a fund for a long period of time doesn't necessarily ensure long-term capital gains. Quite the opposite. Owning an active fund means you will get tax bills each year due to profit taking by the fund manager, and those profits are typically taxed at ordinary income tax rates.

benefit from the lower capital gains tax rate. So regardless of how long you hold the fund, you'll be taxed at your higher ordinary income tax rate.

Why should you care? Because your profits could be slashed by 30% or more, unless you're holding the fund inside a tax-deferred account such as an IRA (individual retirement account) or a 401(k) plan. Not surprisingly, fund companies don't like to dwell on these tax issues, preferring to tout their *pre*tax returns!

Imagine that over time you're losing two-thirds of your potential nest egg to fees—and you're giving up another 30% in unnecessary taxes. How much will *really* be left for your family's future?

So what's the antidote?

Index funds take a "passive" approach that eliminates almost all trading activity. Instead of trading in and out of the market, they simply buy and hold every stock in an index such as the S&P 500. This includes companies like Apple, Alphabet, Microsoft, ExxonMobil, and Johnson & Johnson—currently the five biggest stocks in the S&P 500. Index funds are almost entirely on autopilot: they make very few trades, so their transaction costs and tax bills are incredibly low. They also save a fortune on other expenses. For one thing, they don't have to pay enormous salaries to all those active fund managers and their teams of analysts with Ivy League degrees!

When you own an index fund, you're also protected against all the downright dumb, mildly misguided, or merely unlucky decisions that active fund managers are liable to make. For example, an active manager is likely to keep a portion of the fund's assets in cash, ready to invest if an enticing opportunity arises—or ready to meet redemption requests if lots of investors decide to sell their shares in the fund. Keeping some cash on hand isn't a bad idea, and it's handy when the market falls. But cash doesn't earn a return, so it will underperform stocks over time, assuming that the market continues its general upward trajectory. Ultimately the resulting "cash drag" tends to have a negative impact on the returns of actively managed funds.

What about index funds? Instead of sitting on cash, they remain almost fully invested at all times.

"GOOD LUCK WITH THAT"

Why is it so difficult to time the market successfully, moving in and out of stocks at just the right moment so that you can benefit from the market's upturns and avoid the pain of its downturns? Many people mistakenly assume that you just need to be right a little more than 50% of the time for this approach to pay off. But an exhaustive study by Nobel laureate economist William Sharpe showed that a market-timing investor must be right *69% to 91% of the time*—an impossibly high hurdle.

In another landmark study, researchers Richard Bauer and Julie Dahlquist examined more than a million market-timing sequences from 1926 to 1999. *Their conclusion: just holding the market (via an index fund) outperformed more than 80% of market-timing strategies.*

If you're feeling pissed off right now, I'm with you. You're probably asking yourself: "What the hell am I really getting when I invest in an actively managed fund?" Well, most likely you're buying this toxic brew of human error, high fees, and nasty tax bills! No wonder David Swensen is so skeptical about your chances of achieving financial freedom through active funds. **He warns: "When you look at the results on an after-fee, after-tax basis, over reasonably long periods of time, there's almost no chance that you end up beating the index fund."**

You Get What You Pay For—Except When You Don't

The mutual fund industry is now the world's largest skimming operation, a $7 trillion trough from which fund managers, brokers, and other insiders are steadily siphoning off an excessive slice of the nation's household, college, and retirement savings.

—SENATOR PETER FITZGERALD OF ILLINOIS, cosponsor of the Mutual Fund Reform Act of 2004 (killed by the Senate Banking Committee)

When I was a teenager, I'd sometimes take a girl out to Denny's on a date. I had so little money that I'd order an iced tea and pretend I'd already eaten.

The truth was, I couldn't afford for both of us to eat! The experience of growing up poor left me with a keen awareness of what things *should* cost versus what they *actually* cost. If you go out for a fantastic meal in a great restaurant, you expect it to be expensive. That's fine. But would you pay $20 for a $2 taco? No way! Let me tell you, that's what most people are doing when they invest in actively managed mutual funds.

Have you ever tried to figure out the *actual* fees you pay for the funds you own? If so, you probably zeroed in on the "expense ratio," which covers the fund company's "investment advisory fee," its administrative costs for stuff such as postage and record keeping, plus critical office expenses like free sodas and cappuccinos. A typical fund that invests in stocks might have an expense ratio of 1% to 1.5%. What you probably *didn't* realize is that this is just the start of its fee bonanza!

A few years ago, *Forbes* published a fascinating article entitled "The Real Cost of Owning a Mutual Fund," which revealed just how expensive funds can truly be. As the writer pointed out, you're not only on the hook for the expense ratio, which the magazine estimated conservatively at just less than 1% (0.9%) a year. You're also liable to pay through the nose for "transaction costs" (all those commissions your fund pays whenever it buys or sells stocks), which *Forbes* estimated at 1.44% a year. Then there's the "cash drag," which it estimated at 0.83% a year. And then there's the "tax cost," estimated at 1% a year if the fund is in a taxable account.

The grand total? **If the fund is held in a nontaxable account like a 401(k), you're looking at total costs of 3.17% a year! If it's in a taxable account, the total costs amount to a staggering 4.17% a year!** By comparison, that $20 taco is starting to look like a real bargain!

> You've got to look very carefully at the small print. I don't
> like things that require small print, by the way.
> —JACK BOGLE

I hope you're paying really close attention right now, because the knowledge about all these hidden fees will save you a fortune! But what if you're reading this and thinking "Yeah, but we're only talking about 3% or 4% a year. What's a few percentage points between friends?"

It's true that the numbers look small at first glance. But when you calculate the impact of excessive costs multiplied over many years, it takes your breath away.

Here's another way to put this in perspective: an actively managed fund that charges you 3% a year is *60 times* more expensive than an index fund that charges you 0.05%! Imagine going to Starbucks with a friend. She orders a venti caffé latte and pays $4.15. But you decide that you're happy to pay 60 times more. Your price: $249! I'm guessing you'd think twice before doing that.

In case you think I'm being too extreme, let's consider the example of two neighbors, Joe and David. Both are 35 years old, and each has saved $100,000, which they each decide to invest. Over the next 30 years, the universe smiles on them, and each achieves a gross return of 8% a year. Joe does it by investing in a portfolio of index funds that costs him 0.5% a year in fees. David does it by owning actively managed funds that cost him 2% a year. (I'm being generous here by assuming that the active funds match the performance of the index funds.)

Check out the chart that follows, and you'll see the results. By the age of 65, Joe has seen his nest egg grow from $100,000 to approximately $865,000. As for David, his $100,000 has grown to only $548,000. They both achieved the same rate of return, but they paid different fees. The outcome? Joe has 58% more money—an additional $317,000 for retirement.

As the chart also shows, these two neighbors then start to withdraw $60,000 a year to support themselves in retirement. David runs out of money by the age of 79. But Joe has an entirely different life experience.

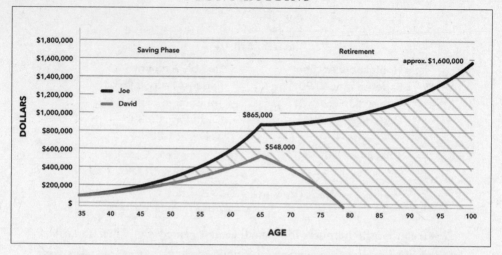

He's able to withdraw $80,000 a year—33% more—and his money lasts until he's 88! Hopefully, Joe lets David live in his basement. For free.

Now do you see why you need to pay such close attention to the fees you're being charged? This one crucial factor might make all the difference between poverty and comfort, misery and joy.

Overpaying for Underperformance: The Five-Star Trap

Here's a question you probably never thought to ask: How do you find an active fund manager who will not only charge you those outrageous fees but also provide you with mediocre returns in exchange? Don't worry. The financial services industry has you covered. If there's one thing in plentiful supply, it's active managers who'll overcharge you for underperformance!

That's the incredible thing. It's not just that actively managed funds are overcharging their customers. It's that their long-term performance is appalling. It's like a double insult. Imagine that you just bought that caffé latte for $249, took a sip, and discovered that the milk had gone bad.

One of the most shocking studies I've seen on this topic of mutual fund performance was by an industry expert named Robert Arnott, the founder of Research Affiliates. He studied all 203 actively managed mutual funds with at least $100 million in assets, tracking their returns for the 15 years from 1984 through 1998. And you know what he found? *Only 8 of these 203 funds actually beat the S&P 500 index.* **That's less than 4%! To put it another way, 96% of these actively managed funds failed to add any value at all over 15 years!**

If you insist on buying an actively managed fund, what you're really betting on is your ability to pick one of the 4 percent that outperformed the market. This reminds me of a gambling analogy that appeared in a *Fast Company* magazine article entitled "The Myth of Mutual Funds." Its authors, Chip and Dan Heath, highlight the absurdity of expecting to pick a fund from that 4% group: "By way of comparison, if you get dealt two face cards in blackjack [each face card is worth 10, so now your total is 20], and your inner idiot shouts, 'Hit me!' you have about an 8% chance of winning."

I don't know about you, but I prefer not to let my inner idiot run the show! So why would I bet on my ability to identify the *tiny* minority of fund managers who'll outperform over many years?

You might be a hard-core researcher who loves to read the *Wall Street Journal* and Morningstar, searching for the illustrious five-star fund—the outperformer. **But there's another problem that few anticipate: today's winners are almost always tomorrow's losers.** The *Wall Street Journal* wrote about one study that went all the way back to 1999 and looked at what happened over the *next* 10 years to all of the top-performing funds that had received a "five-star" rating from Morningstar. What did the researchers discover? "Of the 248 mutual stock funds with five-star ratings at the start of the period, just four still kept that rank after 10 years." The fancy term for this process is "reversion to the mean": a polite way of saying that most highfliers will eventually fall, reverting back to mediocrity.

Unfortunately, many people pick top-rated funds without realizing that they're falling into the trap of buying what's hot—usually right before it turns cold. David Swensen explains: **"Nobody wants to say, 'I own a bunch of one- and two-star funds.' They want to own four-star funds and five-star funds and brag about it at the office. But the four- and five-star funds are the ones that *have* performed well, not the ones that *will* perform well. If you systematically buy the ones that have performed well and sell the ones that have performed poorly, you're going to end up underperforming."**

COULD IT GET ANY WORSE?

Mutual fund companies are notorious for opening lots of funds in hopes that a few of them might outperform. They can then quietly close all the funds that did badly and heavily market the few that did well. After all, they can't sell shoddy past performance, no matter how glossy the brochure. Jack Bogle explains: "A firm will go out and start five incubation funds, and they will try and shoot the lights out with all five of them. And, of course, they don't with four of them, but they do with one. So they drop the other four and take public the one that did very well, with a great track record, and sell that track record."

Bogle adds that, statistically, you're bound to have a few outperformers if you create enough funds: **"Tony, if you pack 1,024 gorillas in a gymnasium and teach them each to flip a coin, one of them will flip heads ten times in a row. Most would call that luck, but when that happens in the fund business, we call him a genius!"**

Does all of this mean it's *impossible* to beat the market over long periods of time? Actually, no. It's extremely hard, but there are a few "unicorns" out there who have outperformed the market by a mile over several decades. These are superstars such as Warren Buffett, Ray Dalio, Carl Icahn, and Paul Tudor Jones, who not only are brilliantly clever but also have ideal temperaments, enabling them to remain calm and rational even when markets are imploding and most people are losing their minds. One reason why they win is that they base every investment decision on a deep understanding of probabilities, not on emotion or desire or luck.

But most of these unicorns run enormous hedge funds that are closed to new investors. For example, Ray Dalio used to accept money from investors who had a net worth of at least $5 billion and who entrusted him with a minimum of $100 million. Nowadays he won't accept *any* new investors, regardless of how many billions you've got hidden under your mattress!

When I asked Ray how hard it is to beat the market over the long run, he didn't pull his punches. "You're not going to beat the market," he told me. "Competing in the markets is more difficult than winning in the Olympics. There are more people who are trying to do it and much bigger rewards if you succeed. Like competing in the Olympics only an infinitesimal percentage succeed, but unlike winning in the Olympics, most people think they can do it. Before you try to beat the market, recognize that your likelihood of being successful is extremely small and ask yourself if you spent the time to train and prepare to be one of the few who actually wins."

You can't ignore it when one of the giants who *has* actually beaten the

market over decades tells you that you shouldn't even bother trying but should stick instead with index funds.

Warren Buffett, who has outpaced the market by a huge margin, also advises regular people to invest in index funds, so they can avoid the drain of excessive fees. To prove his point that almost all active managers underperform index funds over the long run, he made a $1 million bet in 2008 with a New York–based firm called Protégé Partners. He challenged Protégé to select five top hedge fund managers who could collectively beat the S&P 500 over a 10-year period.

So what happened? After 9.5 years, a full 6 months before the bet was officially over, Protégé Partners conceded the bet because it was so lopsided. The Protégé portfolio had returned just 2.2% annually while the S&P 500 had averaged 7.1% annually. In other words, a $1 million investment would have a gained just $220,000 with the hedge fund portfolio while the S&P 500 would have gained $854,000.

Meanwhile, Buffett says he's left instructions that, after his death, the money he leaves in trust for his wife should be invested in low-cost index funds. His explanation? "I believe the trust's long-term results from this policy will be superior to those attained by most investors—whether pension funds, institutions, or individuals—who employ high-fee managers."

Even from his grave, Buffett is absolutely determined to avoid the corrosive effects of high fees!

In his 2016 letter to shareholders, Buffett blasts the wealthy and "sophisticated" for their search for outperformers. He guestimates that "the search by the elite for superior investment advice has caused it, in aggregate, to waste more than $100 billion over the past decade." His rant doesn't stop there: "The wealthy are accustomed to feeling that it is their lot in life to get the best food, schooling, entertainment, housing, plastic surgery, sports ticket, you name it. Their money, they feel, should buy them something superior compared to what the masses receive." (They) have great trouble meekly signing up for a financial product (index funds) or service that is available as well to people investing only a few thousand dollars." More simple yet brilliant guidance from the Oracle of Omaha himself.

Do you remember when I told you earlier that knowledge is merely *potential* power? It's only when you take your knowledge and *act* on it that you possess true power. In this chapter, you've learned what an astounding impact fees can have on your financial future. But what will you *do* with that knowledge? How will you act on it and benefit from it?

Imagine for a moment that you stop buying actively managed funds that charge exorbitant fees. Instead, from now on, you invest only in low-cost index funds. What's the result? At the very least, I would estimate that you can cut your fund expenses by 1% a year. But as you know, that's not the only benefit of switching to index funds. **Hypothetically, let's imagine that your index funds outperform those actively managed funds by 1% annually. In total, you've just added 2% a year to your returns. This alone can give you 20 years of extra retirement income.**[8]

Now do you see how much power you possess to take charge of your financial future? Take that power and use it to dramatically drive down your costs. This will help you immeasurably to become unshakeable!

Meanwhile, let's take a breath. Then let's step into another area where you can save yourself a fortune: your 401(k). Turn the page. . . . We're about to embark on a mission to rescue your retirement account.

---

8 This assumes 2 investors with a starting investment of $100,000 and equal returns of 8% over 30 years, but with 1% fees and 2% fees, respectively. Assuming equal withdrawal amounts at retirement, the investor paying 2% in fees will run out of money 10 years sooner.

CHAPTER 4

RESCUING OUR RETIREMENT PLANS

What Your 401(k) Provider Doesn't Want You to Know

The 401(k) plan was a beautiful invention. Created in 1984, it gave regular people like you and me a chance to build wealth by making tax-deductible contributions to a retirement account directly from our paychecks. What a great concept! You and I were given this opportunity to own a piece of the American dream, to invest in our own futures, to take full responsibility for achieving our own financial freedom. Now nearly 90 million Americans participate in 401(k) plans. To put that in perspective, only 75 million Americans own a home. With more than $6 trillion currently invested in 401(k)s, this is the single most important vehicle for the financial security of the US population.

But you know what happened? Somewhere along the line, the dream got derailed. With trillions of dollars up for grabs, financial firms dreamed up countless ways to dip all of their fingers, thumbs, and toes into the pie. This is the uglier side of our nation's gift for innovation! And it places us under enormous pressure to learn how to protect ourselves from these money grubbers.

You might not believe this, but for almost three decades, the companies providing 401(k) plans were not even required by law to disclose how much they were charging their customers! Only in 2012 did the government finally force these firms to make detailed disclosures of how much they were extracting from your savings. In what other industry would customers tolerate this "Trust me!" style of doing business? Can you imagine a clothing store with no price tags? Can you imagine booking a vacation and leaving it up to the airline and the hotel to decide how much to drain from your bank account without informing you?

Needless to say, financial firms resisted the temptation to take advantage of this lack of disclosure, since they understood that handling our retirement money is a sacred trust. Just kidding! *Of course* they took advantage!

Now that the law has changed, would you guess that the problem has been fixed? Hardly! The whole 401(k) system is *still* a black box. Today financial firms provide disclosure documents that are often 30 to 50 pages long and filled with impenetrable language. Surprise, surprise: not that many people devote their weekends to reading these ultracomplicated documents. Instead of digging through the fine print, most plan participants simply trust that their employers are looking out for them. And most employers are trusting the broker who sold them the plan over a round of golf. **Remember, 71% of people enrolled in 401(k)s think there are *no* fees, and 92% admit that they have no clue what they are! But the truth is, the vast majority of plans are characterized by huge broker commissions, expensive actively managed funds, and layer after layer of additional—and often hidden—charges.**

Robert Hiltonsmith, a senior policy analyst at a think tank called Dēmos, took the trouble to study and decipher the prospectuses of 20 funds in his 401(k) plan. He hacked his way through the forest of bewildering legalese and confusing acronyms, and then wrote a report entitled *The Retirement Savings Drain: The Hidden & Excessive Costs of 401(k)s.* **What did he find? Customers like him—and you and me—were hit with *17* different fees and additional costs!**

Just to be clear, we're not referring here to the absurdly high fees that you're being charged by the mutual funds in your 401(k) plan. It's not enough for you to pay for all those actively managed funds—the ones that *Forbes* says could be costing you 3.17% a year! No, these are the *additional* fees that you're also being charged by the plan provider that's administering your 401(k). These providers are typically insurance or payroll companies—but you might want to think of them as another set of exceptionally well-paid toll collectors.

You've got to hand it to these providers: they're truly ingenious when it comes to dreaming up different ways to siphon off the money in your 401(k)! Here's a short sample of the many categories of fees they've invented: investment expenses, communication expenses, bookkeeping expenses, administrative expenses, trustee expenses, legal expenses, transactional expenses, and stewardship expenses. Why not just add a category called "expense expenses"?

I'm always amazed by what you can find buried in the fine print of providers' disclosure documents—the vague terminology that obscures exactly what's being done to you. For example, you'll often see intentionally meaningless terms such as "net asset charge," "asset-management charge," "contract asset charge," "AMC charge," or "CAC charge." One provider—a leading insurance company—was so brazen as to add a line item called "required revenue." Required by *who*? What for? To pay for the CEO to buy a yacht?

How much does all of this cost you? Hiltonsmith calculated the impact of these additional 401(k) fees on an average worker who earns about $30,000 a year and saves 5% of his or her annual income. Over a lifetime, this worker would lose $154,794 in fees. That's more than five years of income. **A worker who earns about $90,000 a year would lose $277,000 in 401(k) fees**.

You know as well as I do how hard it is for most people to save money for retirement. It requires real sacrifices. But excessive expenses can easily destroy the benefits of all that effort. Some plans take the excessive fees to a whole other level. Certain providers, not content with their typical take, charge a front-end "sales load" on all initial deposits. **One of the worst we have seen takes a whopping 5.75% of every single dollar you sock away. It's like a tithe to the corporate gods running these companies. Add that to the 2% in annual fees they charge, and you're down 7.75% before you're out of the gate.**

Sadly, teachers, nurses, and nonprofit employees are most vulnerable to this huge skimming operation. This is because their 403(b) plans—their equivalent of a 401(k)—aren't covered under the same ERISA (Employee Retirement Income Security Act of 1974) laws that are (at least in theory) designed to protect employees. It makes me sick to think that those who sacrifice the most to make our society better are being screwed by brokers who somehow manage to sleep at night—probably on 2,000-thread-count sheets.

In a *New York Times* article titled "Think Your Retirement Plan Is Bad? Talk to a Teacher," reporter Tara Siegel Bernard does a brilliant job exposing how these poor folks are mugged. In one of the most ghastly scenarios imaginable, "The teachers were each charged a fee of at least 2% of their savings to manage the money, in addition to sales charges of up to 6% each time they made a deposit . . . Moreover, the calculations didn't include the expenses of the dozens of mutual funds they were invested in, some of which exceeded 1%."

That's 9% in first-year expenses alone. That's not a hole in your boat. That's the whole back of the boat ripped off and dragging in the water.

This is why it's so important to be aware of how the financial industry stacks the odds against you. Knowledge is your first defense. After all, how can you protect yourself from a threat to your financial well-being unless you *know* that this threat exists?

One person who shares my outrage about 401(k) expenses is the comedian John Oliver, who investigated the subject for his HBO show *Last Week Tonight with John Oliver*. When the members of his research team dissected their own 401(k) plan, they discovered that their provider's fees amounted to 1.69% a year, *excluding* the exorbitant fees they were also being charged to invest in the actively managed funds in their plan. **Oliver explains how "seemingly tiny fees can mount up" until "you've lost almost two-thirds of what you would have had." He warns: "Think of fees like termites: they're tiny, they're barely noticeable, and they can eat away your f———g future."**

HEADS I WIN, TAILS YOU LOSE

What makes all of this so upsetting is that a 401(k) *should* be—and *can* be—a powerful tool for building wealth, if it's used correctly. Instead, the vast majority of plans are riddled with opaque fee arrangements and conflicts of interest. In 2015 the Obama administration announced that "hidden fees and backdoor payments" were costing Americans more than $17 billion per year. And Secretary of Labor Thomas E. Perez has said, "The corrosive power of fine print and buried fees can eat away like a chronic illness at a person's savings."

In early 2016 Congress passed new laws designed to force 401(k) providers to act in their clients' best interests. Sadly, the rules were never fully implemented because the incoming administration decided to kill the regulations. So who knows if rules that prioritize your best interests will ever see the light of day. It's now 2018 and 401(k) brokers can still charge commissions, sell you their own name-brand funds and whack you with front-end loaded sales charges. Business as usual.

If you ask me, one of the worst abuses is that nearly all of the big-name providers routinely accept payments from the mutual funds they offer in 401(k) plans. **This legal but grubby arrangement is called revenue sharing, or "pay to play."** It's the equivalent of buying shelf space in a store to ensure that it will stock a crappy product that shoppers really ought to avoid.

What's the result? **Many of the funds you get to choose from in your 401(k) plan are on the list only because the fund company paid the provider to include them! These funds tend to be actively managed, so they're expensive. And they're rarely the best performers. In some cases, they even charge a "front-end load": a fee that often amounts to 3% of your assets just to buy the fund in the first place.**

So why not just pick low-cost index funds when you're investing in your 401(k) plan? Great question! The trouble is, most providers make index funds available only if the plan has a high level of assets. Why? Because index funds aren't sufficiently lucrative for the provider. So they prefer

to exclude them from the menu, if they can get away with it. **If you work for a smaller company, chances are that you'll be *forced* to invest in funds with higher fees.** In fact, 93% of 401(k) plans have less than $5 million in total plan assets. These are small and midsized companies that don't have the buying power to demand better investment options for their employees. Yet it's entirely unfair to penalize people for working at smaller companies.

Some 401(k) providers do offer index funds to smaller plans, but they typically charge a significant markup. **One major insurance company is offering an S&P 500 index fund for 1.68% annually, when the actual cost is just 0.05%. *That's a 3,260% markup!*** Think of it this way: your friend buys a Honda Accord for the regular retail price of $22,000. But you're forced to pay a 3,260% markup. Your cost for the exact same car: $717,200! Welcome to the world of high finance.

Another well-known insurance company charges a 3% sales load to buy a Vanguard index fund, and then charges 0.65% a year in fees for the fund—a steal at a mere 1,300% markup. This is the white-collar equivalent of ruthless mobsters coming round to your small business and hitting you up for protection money. The only justification is that *you* have money, and *they* want it.

Meanwhile, some providers will allow you to open your own "self-directed" 401(k) account if you want access to low-cost index funds or want to manage your own investments. Sounds like a good option, right? One friend of mine thought so. He opened a self-directed account, bought some index funds, and congratulated himself on bypassing all the ridiculously expensive funds in his plan. Then he found out that the provider was charging him an additional 1.9% a year for the privilege of using a self-directed account! In other words, heads you lose, tails I win.

These tricks of the trade are, at last, coming back to haunt many 401(k) providers. As I write this, at least ten major providers have been sued by their employees for charging excessive fees in their own 401(k) plans! One of the biggest 401(k) providers settled two class-action lawsuits for $12 million after accusations by its own employees that its 401(k) fees were too high. Imagine going to a restaurant and discovering that the waiters and kitchen staff refuse to eat the chef's food! When the insiders don't like what their company is selling, should you and I just smile politely and accept that it's good enough for the likes of us?

One reason why I feel so passionate about this is that I've experienced firsthand how easy it is to get exploited by unscrupulous 401(k) providers. When I began to see these widespread abuses at companies across America, I called the head of human resources at one of my companies to learn more about the plan we were providing for our employees. I think of them as family, and I wanted to make sure we were treating them with all the care they deserve.

To my horror, I discovered that our name-brand 401(k) plan—administered by a major insurance company—was loaded with expensive mutual funds, excessive "administrative expenses," and fat commissions that we paid to the broker who sold us the plan. It turned out that the total expenses in our 401(k) plan amounted to 2.17% a year. Over time these fees would erode much of the money that our employees were saving scrupulously for their future. I was beside myself.

So I began to look around for a solution. After much investigation, I was introduced by a friend to Tom Zgainer, CEO of a company called America's Best 401k (ABk). As you'd imagine, I was more than a little skeptical. Why should I believe that his firm would live up to its less-than-modest name? But it didn't take long to realize that he's a truth teller who's determined to challenge his industry's unseemly practices. **As Tom told me, the 401(k) business is "the largest dark pool of assets where nobody really knows how or whose hands are getting greased."**

By contrast, ABk is entirely transparent. For example, he has no interest in the sordid pay-to-play game. **Instead of accepting kickbacks from mutual fund companies that want him to sell their overpriced funds, he offers only inexpensive index funds from firms such as Vanguard and Dimensional Fund Advisors. Tom's company charges one fee—with no markups or hidden costs. It's a fully bundled solution that eliminates brokers, commissions, and high-paid middlemen.**

I'm delighted to tell you that I quickly and easily moved my company's old plan into a new plan administered by America's Best 401k. The total costs for our new 401(k) plan—including investment expenses, investment management services, and record-keeping fees—add up to a grand total of just 0.65% a year. That's a savings of about 70% in our annual expenses. **Over the years, this should put as much as $5 million back into the pockets of my employees. And Tom charges nothing for companies to make the switch.**

I was so impressed that I referred many other friends to ABk. To my delight, they were all thrilled. No wonder. **Tom's firm saves his average client more than 57% in fees**! I got excited and decided to partner with Tom on his mission to rescue the retirement plans of millions of people. It's time to break the ruthless chokehold this industry has on our families' financial futures.

Whether you are a business owner or an employee, you can see how your company's 401(k) plan stacks up by visiting **www.ShowMeTheFees.com**. It only takes a few minutes and they will show how much you are really paying in fees, what the impact those fees will have over time and if there is a significant savings opportunity. All they require is a copy of your current fee disclosure document and they will tell you exactly where to locate it depending on your current provider (typically available on the plan website). Most of the time, the savings can amount to hundreds of thousands, even millions, that will go back into the pockets of the plan participants and their families! Employees can also share this report with their employer (or the HR department) to help spur a change for the better.

I was chatting about this with my dentist and friend Dr. Craig Spodak. He has more than 40 employees, and he wanted to make sure they weren't being ripped off. I don't want to name specific names here because these problems are systemic, not just limited to a handful of companies. But when Craig told me the name of the infamous company that provided his 401(k) plan, I couldn't help but cringe. My diagnosis was immediate: his dentistry practice would need to undergo an urgent extraction. Otherwise the pain would only get worse.

I put Craig in contact with my partners at America's Best 401k. In a matter of minutes, he emailed them his plan's "fee disclosure" form, and they drilled down to expose his fees. He was shocked by the results. It turned out that his plan contained a long list of overpriced mutual funds and an additional layer of bloated "contract asset charges." The total costs he and his employees paid for this terrible plan were north of 2.5% a year! Suddenly Craig understood why his broker used to bring him donuts as a gift—and why the man was always grinning from ear to ear!

You won't be surprised to hear that Craig fired his broker, dumped his provider, and entrusted his plan instead to America's Best 401k.

As you can see in the box below, employers need to wake up—just as Craig and I did—so they can ensure that their employees aren't being exploited. Otherwise there could be a high price to pay, not just for the employees but also for the employer.

If you're an employee, after you use the Fee Checker, you can forward the report to your company's owner or to senior management. Once they know the truth about what's going on, they may well want to improve your 401(k) plan. After all, their financial future is also at stake.

BUSINESS OWNERS BEWARE! TAKE 3 MINUTES TO DISCOVER HOW YOU CAN ELIMINATE LEGAL LIABILITIES AND PROTECT YOURSELF AND YOUR COMPANY FROM NEW DEPARTMENT OF LABOR FINES:

If you own or run a company that offers a 401(k) plan, you're officially regarded as the plan's "sponsor"—whether you know it or not. That means it's your legal obligation to act as the "fiduciary" to your plan and to your employees, which means that you have to operate in their best interests. If you trip up, you could easily find yourself with a major liability that could damage your business and even your own finances. It's a bit like owning a house that's structurally unsound: you might be fine for years—until you're not. So, ignore this at your peril!

What do you have to do? First, you need to demonstrate to the Department of Labor (DOL) that you're taking the necessary steps to fulfill your role as the plan's sponsor. This includes periodically benchmarking your plan against other plans to ensure that the fees being charged in your plan are reasonable. Most business owners I talk to have no idea about this obligation. **This potentially exposes them to the mighty wrath of the DOL. In 2014 the department determined that 75% of the plans it examined were illegal. The average fine: _$600,000_.**

And that's just the beginning. You're also exposed to the risk that your own employees could sue you personally. In 2015 the US Supreme Court issued a major ruling against Edison International, the power giant. This decision should make it easier for 401(k) plan participants to sue their employers for choosing investments with excessive fees. Small businesses are particularly vulnerable—not just because it's hard for them to afford hefty fines but also because they tend to have small 401(k) plans, which typically charge the highest fees.

One practical step that could save you a fortune is to contact my partners at America's Best 401k and ask them to provide you with a free benchmark for your plan. All it takes is a few minutes to furnish them with the fee disclosure statement for your plan. **The fact that you've obtained this benchmark demonstrates to the DOL that you've taken your legal responsibility seriously**. Even better, many companies discover that they can easily cut their plan's fees in half—or more. If so, that will endow you and your employees with a huge windfall for many years to come.

www.showmethefees.com

Where are we headed next? Before we turn our focus to your investment playbook, we've got one more invaluable lesson to cover: how to find sophisticated, conflict-free financial advice that will turbocharge your journey to financial success.

You'll learn how to avoid all those salespeople in disguise who get rich by dishing out so-called advice that benefits them, not you. As you'll see, choosing the right advisor can mean the difference between poverty and wealth, between insecurity and freedom. The choice is yours.

So let's find out: Who can you really trust?

CHAPTER 5

WHO CAN YOU REALLY TRUST?

Pulling Back the Curtain on the Tricks of the Trade

It is difficult to get a man to understand something when
his salary depends on his not understanding it.

—UPTON SINCLAIR

When I ask people how they're doing, the most common answer I get is: "Busy." We're all running faster than ever these days. So it's no surprise that more and more of us are hiring financial advisors to help us navigate the complicated journey to financial freedom. From 2010 to 2015, the percentage of the US population using financial advisors doubled. **In fact, more than 40% of Americans now use an advisor. And the more money you have, the more likely you are to seek out advice: 81% of people with more than $5 million have an advisor.**

But how do you find an advisor you trust—and who *deserves* your trust?

It's astonishing how many people *don't* trust the person giving them financial advice! **A 2016 survey by the Certified Financial Planner Board of Standards found that 60% of respondents "believe that financial advisors act in their companies' best interests rather than the consumers' best interests."** That figure had soared from 25% since 2010.[9] **To put that in perspective, Congress currently has a dismal 20% approval rating,**[10]

9 "Participant Trust and Engagement Study," National Association of Retirement Plan Participants (2016), www.ireachcontent.com/news-releases/consumer-trust-in-financial -institutions-hits-an-all-time-low-575677131.html.

10 "Congressional Job Approval Ratings Trend (1974–Present)," Gallup.com.

but just *10%* of Americans surveyed trust financial institutions. It's hard to think of any other industry where customers feel so suspicious—except perhaps the used-car business.

What accounts for this epidemic of distrust? Well, it's not easy to place your full faith and confidence in an industry that's constantly in the news for yet another scandal. **Check out the "Hall of Shame" table below, and you'll see that 10 of the world's largest financial firms have had to fork out $179.5 billion in legal settlements just in the seven years from 2009 through 2015.** Between them, America's four largest banks—Bank of America, JPMorgan Chase, Citigroup, and Wells Fargo—made 88 *settlements* amounting to a total of *$145.84 billion*!

Hall of Shame
Table of Corporate Settlements

Company	Total Settlements	Sums paid ($ billions)
Bank of America	34	$77.09 billion
JPMorgan Chase	26	$40.12 billion
Citigroup	18	$18.39 billion
Wells Fargo	10	$10.24 billion
BNP Paribas	1	$8.90 billion
UBS	8	$6.54 billion
Deutsche Bank	4	$5.53 billion
Morgan Stanley	7	$4.78 billion
Barclays	7	$4.23 billion
Credit Suisse	4	$3.74 billion

Source: Keefe, Bruyette & Woods

Some of the stories behind these settlements are so outrageous that they make you shake your head in wonder. Here's a sample of four typical newspaper headlines just from the last few months:

- "Bank of America to Pay $415 Million to Settle SEC Probe": the *Wall Street Journal* reports that the bank's Merrill Lynch brokerage unit "misused customer cash and securities to generate profits" for itself, putting at risk up to $58 billion in client assets!

- "Citigroup Fined in Rate-Rigging Inquiry but Avoids Criminal Charges": the *New York Times* reports that the bank was fined $425 million for manipulating benchmark interest rates from 2007 to 2012. Citigroup's motive: "to benefit its own trading positions at the expense of its trading partners' and clients'."

- "Ex-Barclays Employees Guilty of LIBOR Rigging": *USA Today* reports that three former Barclays employees conspired "to manipulate a global financial benchmark used to set rates on trillions of dollars of mortgages and other loans." Did you get that? That's *trillions*, with a *T*!

- "Wells Fargo Fined $185M for Fraudulently Opening Accounts": the *New York Times* reports that employees of the bank "opened roughly 1.5 million bank accounts and applied for 565,000 credit cards" *without customer consent*! The bank fired at least 5,300 employees involved in this scandal.

How can you place your financial future in the hands of people who work in an industry with this *demonstrated* record of putting its own interests above those of its clients? How can you expect them not to deceive, exploit, and abuse you?

After all, these companies aren't fringe operators with fly-by-night reputations. These are—or *were*—some of the most respected and most blue-chip behemoths in this business! For example, Wells Fargo had long been celebrated as one of the best-run banks in the world. Yet its CEO was forced to resign in shame over his firm's opening of fake bank accounts, forfeiting $41 million in stock options that he'd received as a reward for his performance.

Now, let me be absolutely clear. I'm not criticizing any individuals who work in this field or for these specific firms. I'd be surprised if the CEO of Wells Fargo truly knew about this widespread wrongdoing within his massive company, which has more than a quarter million employees. Policing companies this enormous has become an almost impossible challenge for some. I have lots of friends and clients in the financial industry, so I'm speaking with firsthand knowledge when I tell you that they—and the vast majority of their colleagues—are people of real integrity. They have good hearts and good intentions.

The trouble is, they work in a system that's beyond their control—a system that has tremendously powerful financial incentives to focus on maximizing profits above all else. This is a system that richly rewards employees who put their employer's interests first, their own interests second, and their clients' interests a distant third. And for folks like you and me, that's a recipe for disaster—unless we take the precaution of learning how the system works against us, and how to counter it.

"YOU CAN TRUST ME" . . . TO TAKE ADVANTAGE OF YOU!

Before we go any further, it's worth explaining where financial advisors fit within this profit-hungry system—and what exactly they do. They operate in a realm where nothing is quite what it seems to be. So it's fitting that they go by many different names, which often seem downright misleading!

According to the *Wall Street Journal*, there are more than 200 different designations for financial advisors, including "financial consultants," "wealth managers," "financial advisors," "investment consultants," "wealth advisors," and (in case that doesn't sound exclusive enough) "private wealth advisors." These are all just different ways of saying "I'm respectable! I'm professional! Of *course*, you can trust me!"

Regardless of the title, what you really need to know is that 90% of the roughly 310,000 financial advisors in America are actually just brokers. In other words, they're paid to sell financial products to customers like you and me in return for a fee.

Why does this matter? Because brokers have a vested interest in hawking expensive products, which might include actively managed mutual funds, whole life insurance policies, variable annuities, and wrap accounts. These products typically pay them a onetime sales commission or, even better (for them), ongoing annual fees. A broker at a major firm might be required to produce at least $500,000 a year in sales. So it doesn't matter how fancy the title sounds: these are salespeople under intense pressure to generate revenues. If calling themselves a financial consultant or a private wealth advisor helps them reach their aggressive sales targets, so be it. If calling themselves a wizard, a pixie, or an elf helped more, that'd be just fine, too.

Does this mean they're dishonest? Not at all. But it *does* mean they're working for the house. And remember: the house always wins. There's a good chance your broker is a sincere person with high integrity, but he's selling what he's been trained to sell—and you should always assume that whatever he's selling will benefit the house first. **Sophisticated customers know this is standard operating procedure: one survey found that 42% of ultrawealthy clients think their advisor is more concerned with selling products than with helping them!**

Warren Buffett jokes that you never want to ask a barber whether you need a haircut. Well, brokers are the barbers of the financial world. They're trained and incentivized to sell, regardless of whether you need what they're selling! That's not a criticism. It's just a fact.

I also want to make it clear that I'm not out to criticize or demonize the financial firms that employ these brokers. Have these companies done their fair share of stupid, unethical, and illegal things? You bet. But they're not evil or malicious. **They never set out to sabotage the global economic** system! These companies simply do what they're incentivized to do, which is to meet shareholders' needs. And what do shareholders need? Bigger profits. And what creates bigger profits? More fees. If there's a legally grey area that these companies can exploit to generate those additional fees, they're likely to do it because that's what they're *incentivized* to do.

You might expect all those enormous legal settlements to act as a deterrent, encouraging these companies to improve their behavior. **But these penalties are paltry for such colossal businesses. Bank of America had to shell out $415 million in fines for misusing its customers' assets. Big deal! In one three-month period in 2015, the bank earned a profit of $5.3 *billion*. That's in just 12 weeks! For companies this rich, those pesky fines are just a routine cost of doing business—the equivalent of you or me getting a parking ticket.**

Instead of changing their ways, these companies focus much of their effort on burnishing their brands through slick ad campaigns featuring dreamy images of sailboats and romantic walks on the beach. Why am I telling you this? Because we're conditioned to trust brands. We need to break free from this conditioning and look with more critical eyes at the reality, not the illusion. Otherwise how can we safeguard ourselves against this powerful system that's fueled by self-interest?

It makes me angry and sad that the financial system is so broken. But anger and sadness won't protect you from getting ripped off. What *will* protect you is knowing how the system can work against you. **If you don't understand the incentives of your advisor, you're liable to discover that you've done wonders for *his* financial future while potentially wrecking your own.**

This chapter will show you how to navigate the minefield. You'll learn to distinguish between three different types of advisors so you can sidestep the salespeople and choose a fiduciary who is *required by law* to act in your best interests. We'll also give you the criteria to judge whether a particular advisor is right or wrong for you, based on fact, not on how likeable he or she is. After all, it's easy to be persuaded by people you like, especially when they are sincere. Remember, people can be sincere—and sincerely wrong.

Maybe you're wondering if you need an advisor at all. If you decide to manage your own finances, this book and *Money: Master the Game* will set you on the right track so you can achieve your financial goals. But in my experience, the best financial advisors can add extraordinary value by helping you with everything from investing, to taxes, to insurance. They provide holistic advice that's truly invaluable. If you're not convinced, check out Vanguard's study below.

For me, getting first-rate advice has been a game changer, saving me a tremendous amount of money and time. I'm a capable guy, and I pride myself on understanding the most important principles in anything I'm a part of, but I'm not about to do brain surgery on myself!

SKEPTICAL ABOUT THE VALUE OF THE RIGHT ADVISOR?

While the wrong advisors can be detrimental to your financial health, the right ones can be worth their value in gold. A recent Vanguard study explored exactly how much monetary value an advisor can bring to your investments.

- Lowering expense ratios: 45 basis points (0.45%) back in your pocket
- Rebalancing portfolio: 35 basis points (0.35%) of increased performance
- Asset allocation: 75 basis points (0.75%) of increased performance
- Withdrawing the right investments in retirement: 70 basis points (0.70%) in savings
- Behavioral coaching: 150 basis points (1.50%) for serving as your practical psychologist

The grand total: 3.75% of added value! **That's more than three times what a sophisticated advisor would charge.** And heck, that doesn't include reducing taxes and more.

Francis M. Kinniry Jr. et al., *Putting a Value on Your Value: Quantifying Vanguard Advisor's Alpha*, Vanguard Research (September 2016).

A LOSING BET

One of these is not like the other.

—BIG BIRD

Did you ever have that unsettling suspicion that someone wasn't telling you the "whole" truth, but you couldn't quite put your finger on why you didn't trust the person or how exactly he or she might be lying to you? It's a familiar feeling when you're searching for financial advice. How can you tell if the person offering you "help" is the real deal? And how can you even know where to start, when so many different people with so many different titles are offering you potential solutions?

In the interests of cutting through the confusion, I'm going to make this as simple and straightforward as possible. *In reality, all financial advisors fall into just one of three categories.* **What you really need to know is whether your advisor is:**

- **a broker,**
- **an independent advisor, or**
- **a dually registered advisor.**

Now let's break this down in more detail so you know exactly what you're dealing with.

Brokers

As I mentioned earlier, about 90% of all financial advisors in America are brokers, regardless of the title on their business card. They're paid a fee or commission for selling products. Many of them work for enormous Wall Street banks, brokerage houses, and insurance companies—the kind that splash their names on sports arenas.

How do you know if the product a broker recommends is the best one for you? **Let me clear it up. Brokers don't have to recommend the best product for you.** What?! Yes, you heard me right. All they're obliged to do is follow what's known as the "suitability" standard. That means they must simply believe that any recommendations they make are "suitable" for their clients.

Suitability is an *extremely* low bar to clear. Do you dream of marrying a *suitable* person or your soul mate? But for a broker, suitable is good enough.

The problem is, brokers and their employers earn more by recommending certain products. For example, an actively managed fund with high expenses will be far more lucrative for the broker and the brokerage house than a low-cost index fund, which will be far more lucrative for you and your family. Does it sound to you like there's a serious conflict of interest here? Damn right!

How is it that profits over people has become the accepted standard? To put this in context, the United Kingdom has a fiduciary standard, which means that *all* financial advisors are required by law to act in their clients' best interests. Australia also has a fiduciary standard. So why aren't American professionals obliged to act as fiduciaries? Actually, they are—except for financial professionals. Doctors, lawyers, and certified public accountants in the United States are legally required to act in the best interests of the people they help. Yet financial advisors get a free pass!

There have been many attempts to enact laws requiring advisors to serve their clients' best interests. But the financial industry has lobbied hard to block these laws. Why? **Frankly, advisors and their employers would earn way less money if they could no longer stack the deck in their favor.** Imagine their horror if they could no longer hawk their own overpriced products, or collect substantial commissions and secret kickbacks such as revenue-sharing deals from other companies.

One piece of (moderately) good news is that the Department of Labor recently passed a new regulation requiring advisors to put their clients' interests first in one specific situation: when handling 401(k) and IRA retirement accounts. But even then, there are still major loopholes.[11] In addition, with the recent election of Donald Trump, his advisors are all talking about

11 If you're working with a broker, at some point you'll probably receive a phone call or a letter asking you to sign a "best interest contract exemption," or BICE. The broker may tell you, "The government passed a ridiculous law that limits your choices. If you sign this form, I can continue offering you a full menu of options." Don't fall for it. This is code for "Please sign this form so I can keep selling you my firm's most profitable products and collecting big commissions!"

rolling back the new regulations before they're even implemented. So by the time you read this, those protections may not even exist!

Here's the bottom line: this system is so riddled with conflicts of interest that it puts you in a highly vulnerable position. But what if you're already working with a broker you like and trust?

I'm not suggesting that it's impossible to find talented, trustworthy brokers who do a fine job. **But playing a game where the odds are so heavily stacked against you isn't an intelligent move.** The most successful investors—and even professional gamblers—always try to make sure the odds are on their side. How can the odds be on your side if your broker has a hidden financial agenda? David Swensen, Yale's investment guru, warned me that no matter how much you may like your broker, "Your broker is *not* your friend."

"WHO'S TO SAY MY BEST FRIEND CAN'T ALSO BE MY FINANCIAL ADVISER?"

Registered Investment Advisors

Of 308,937 financial advisors in the United States, *only 31,000*—approximately 10%—are registered investment advisors[12] (also known as RIAs or independent advisors). Like doctors and lawyers, they have a fiduciary duty and a legal obligation to act in their clients' best interests at *all* times. It's simple common sense, right? But in the strange twilight zone of the financial industry, it's anything but common.

To give you a sense of how strong the laws are, if your RIA tells you to buy Apple in the morning, and he buys it for himself at a cheaper price in the afternoon, he has to give you *his* stock! Try asking your broker to do that! In addition, before doing business with you, your RIA must disclose any conflicts of interest and explain up front how he or she is paid. No hocus pocus, nothing hidden, no tricks, no lies, all cards on the table!

Why would you ever choose a financial advisor who *doesn't* have to act in your best interests over one who *does*? You wouldn't! Yet most people do just that! One reason is that they simply don't know any better. The fact that you're reading this book puts you in an elite group—one that understands the fundamental rules of this high-stakes game. Another reason why so many people use brokers is that RIAs are like rare birds: there's only a one-in-ten chance of spotting one.

How come there are so few RIAs, if this is such a superior model? The most obvious reason is that brokers tend to earn a lot more money. All those fat fees from selling financial products can be extremely lucrative. **By contrast, RIAs don't accept sales commissions.** Instead, they typically charge a flat fee for financial advice, or a percentage of their clients' assets under management. It's a cleaner model that removes awkward conflicts of interest.

Dually Registered Advisors

When I first learned about the difference between brokers and RIAs, everything seemed so clear and simple to me! You undoubtedly want someone

12 Fidelity Institutional Asset Management.

who'll act in your best interests, right? So it seemed obvious to insist on working with an independent advisor who's legally obliged to act as a fiduciary. I thought of fiduciaries as the gold standard. But then I discovered that this subject is murkier than I'd realized!

Here's the problem: the vast majority of independent advisors are registered as *both* fiduciaries *and* brokers. WTF?! In fact, as many as 26,000 out of 31,000 RIAs operate in this grey area where they have one foot in both camps. That's right: only 5,000 of the nation's 310,000 financial advisors are pure fiduciaries. **That's a measly 1.6%. Now you know why it's so hard to get unconflicted and transparent advice.**

When I wrote *Money: Master the Game*, I became a champion of fiduciaries, only to discover this inconvenient truth about dual registration, first brought to me by Peter Mallouk.

It infuriated me to learn how these "dual registrants" actually operate. One moment, they play the part of an independent advisor, reassuring you that they abide by the fiduciary standard and can provide you with conflict-free advice for a fee. A second later, they switch hats and act as a broker, earning commissions by selling you products. When they're playing this broker role, they no longer have to abide by the fiduciary standard. In other words, they're sometimes obliged to serve your best interests and sometimes not! How warped is that?

How are you supposed to tell which hat they're wearing at any given moment? Believe me, it's not easy. I've had the experience of asking an advisor if he was a fiduciary and having him look me in the eye and assure me that he was. He talked to me about how untrustworthy brokers are and how much better it is to be a fiduciary. He told me that our interests were perfectly aligned. Then I discovered that he was *also* acting as a broker, since he was dually registered, and it turned out that he made all sorts of side deals that earned him loads of commissions! Here was a person I thought I could recommend as a fiduciary, and he lied to my face. Still, he hadn't broken any laws. I was furious when I realized how easy it is to get misled.

Ironically, most dual registrants were originally brokers who gave up corner offices and sizeable incomes to make the leap to becoming RIAs. They wanted complete independence, to be able to provide their clients with the full range of investment options—not just the carefully crafted menu of products that their previous employer imposed. They wanted to wear the white hat and not the black hat. And so they took the risk and made the jump to RIA, only to discover the sad truth that it's financially really hard to be a pure fiduciary.

These dually registered advisors have good intentions, but they get caught between two worlds, trying to be honorable while also having to make compromises. It's not the fault of the individuals; it's that the industry is structured so that selling products is the easiest way to make good money and pay the bills.

A LITTLE RESPECT

I'm about to give you all of my money / And all I'm
askin' in return, honey / Is for a little respect.
—ARETHA FRANKLIN, "Respect"

By now, you've learned some key facts that will save you a lot of suffering and sorrow. You know that 90% of financial advisors are really just brokers in disguise. You know that they don't have to put your interests first. You know that they're under tremendous pressure to peddle overpriced products. You know that the odds of finding good advice improve dramatically if you steer clear of all brokers—however unfair that seems—and work instead with independent advisors who have a fiduciary duty to put your interests first. You know that all fiduciaries are *not* created equal, since some can suddenly mutate into brokers.

So now you know what to avoid. We've eliminated about 98% of all the advisors out there, on the grounds that they're either brokers or dually registered hybrids. What are you left with? Thousands of independent advisors who are legally obligated to act as fiduciaries. It shouldn't be too difficult to find one who meets your needs.

But you *still* have to tread carefully. Why? Because conflicts of interest can arise even when you're working with an independent advisor—typically involving clever but legal schemes to make additional money off you while you're looking the other way. Here are three tricks of the trade you should watch out for:

The Poison of Proprietary Funds

Brokers routinely sell proprietary funds created by their own firm. It's a not-so-subtle strategy for keeping fees in the family—a common money-making scheme that depends on clients being naïve enough not to ask whether another firm might offer better or cheaper funds. It's just the kind of self-serving behavior that should make you wary of working with brokers. But I'm sorry to tell you that many independent advisors have also figured out furtive ways to use this ruse.

Here's how it typically works: the advisory firm has two arms, one of which is a registered investment advisor that offers independent advice. So far, so good. But the firm's *second* arm is a sister company that owns and operates a bunch of proprietary mutual funds. The RIA pretends to offer impartial advice but actually recommends that you buy the overpriced funds sold by its sister company! As *Saturday Night Live*'s Church Lady would say, "How conveeeenient!" The great thing is that all the profits stay in house, which is better for everyone—oh, except for the client.

The poor client (we might as well call him the *mark*) pays the advisor twice: for "independent" advice on which investments to own *and* for the parent company's own mediocre funds. Most clients aren't even aware that they're buying funds owned by the same firm. That's because the fund arm and the advisory arm typically operate under different brand names. It's like watching a master pickpocket at work. The trickery is so sly and cynical that you almost have to admire it.

An Additional Fee for Doing Nothing

Here's another scheme that's become increasingly common: you pay an advisor a fee to manage your money—let's say, 1% of your assets. The advisor then recommends a "model portfolio" (he may even give it a fancy name like the "XYZ Portfolio Series"), which has its own additional fee—let's say, 0.25% of your assets. This fee is over and above the cost of the underlying investments in your portfolio.

But nothing *additional* is being done for you: the "model portfolio" consists of various investments the advisor has assembled, which is what you paid him to do in the first place. It's like buying $100 worth of groceries and then getting slapped with a $25 fee for the right to carry them out of the store in a paper bag!

If an advisor charges a money management fee for selecting investments, that should be it. End of story. Why should they be able to add *another* fee for pooling those investments together? I'll tell you why: because they can. Because you might not notice.

"I Can't Accept a Commission, So Let's Just Call It a 'Consulting Fee!'"

Some independent advisors make private deals with investment firms that enable the advisor to earn commissions without you knowing it. Here's how it works: your advisor recommends the funds of a specific mutual fund company. The advisor can't do anything so tawdry as receiving a backdoor commission from the fund company in return for recommending its products. This presents a terrible conundrum for the advisor. What to do? Easy! Call this payoff something else!

So the ingenious advisor approaches the fund company and asks instead for a "consulting fee." The fund company gladly pays this fee, and everyone lives happily ever after. Except for you, the client, who just got duped into thinking that you were actually getting "independent" advice. What's the moral? If it walks like a duck and talks like a duck, it's probably a duck. Or a broker.

HOW TO FIND THE BEST ADVISOR FOR YOUR NEEDS

Competence is such a rare bird in these woods
that I appreciate it whenever I see it.
—FRANK UNDERWOOD, *House of Cards*

I hope it's clear by now that your best bet is to hire an independent advisor who's a true fiduciary. But how do you select a specific advisor who makes sense for *you*?

As you can see from the quadrant on the following page, not all fiduciaries are created equal. It's not enough to find someone who's legally obliged

Not All Fiduciaries Are Created Equal

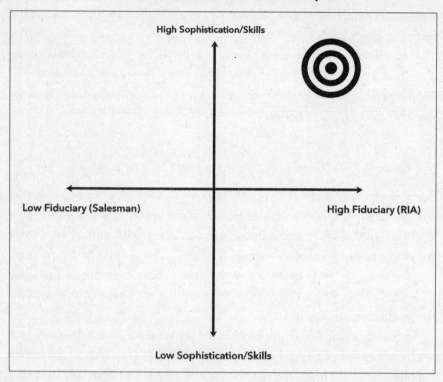

to put your interests first. You also need someone who is financially sophisticated and highly skilled. In other words, your fiduciary should fit in the top right corner of the quadrant: high fiduciary with high sophistication. That's the diametric opposite of the lower left corner, which is a salesperson with low sophistication.

How can you tell if a particular fiduciary has the right skills and experience for you? When you're selecting and vetting them, you can apply the following five criteria:

1. **First, Check Out the Advisor's Credentials.** You need to make sure that the person, or someone on her team, has the right qualifications for the job you need done. We're not talking about fancy titles here. I mean actual professional credentials. If you're looking for planning help, make sure the advisor has a certified financial planner (CFP) on

the team. If you're looking for legal help, make sure there are estate planning attorneys on the team. Looking for tax advice? Make sure there are CPAs on the team.

These credentials aren't a guarantee of high-level skills. Even so, it's important to know that any advisor you're considering has reached the minimum level of competency required to advise in the relevant field.

2. **Ideally, If You're Using an Advisor, You Should Be Getting More Than Just Someone to Design Your Investment Strategy.** What you really need is someone who can help you as the years go by to grow your overall wealth by showing you how to save money on your mortgage, insurance, taxes, and so on—someone who can also help you to design and protect your legacy. **That might sound unnecessary right now, but it's important to have this breadth of expertise, since taxes alone can make a difference of 30% to 50% in what you retain from your investments today!**

I find it ironic when I see ads for wealth management, and all they're doing is designing a portfolio. It's best to start with a person you're going to grow with through time. So make sure he has the resources to grow with you even if you're starting small. Also keep in mind, size does matter. You don't want to end up with a sincere but inexperienced advisor who manages only a relatively tiny sum for a few dozen clients.

3. **Next, You Want to Make Sure Your Advisor Has Experience in Working with People Just Like You.** Does she have the track record to prove she's performed well for clients in your position, with your needs? For example, if your main focus is on building wealth so you can retire, you want a real expert in retirement planning. **Yet in an anonymous survey, the *Journal of Financial Planning* found that 46% of advisors had no retirement plan of their own! I can't believe they admitted this! Can you imagine hiring a personal trainer who hasn't exercised in decades or a nutritionist who's pounding down Twinkies while telling you to eat vegetables?**

4. **It's Also Important to Make Sure That You and Your Advisor Are Aligned Philosophically.** For example, does he believe he can beat the market over the long run by picking individual stocks or actively managed funds? Or does he recognize that the odds of beating the

market are low, leading him to focus on selecting a well-diversified portfolio of index funds? Some advisors might meet your need for a true fiduciary but still fall short because they're determined to pick stocks. Personally, I'd run a mile from any advisor who claims to beat the market regularly. Maybe it's true, but I doubt it. More likely, he's too optimistic or is lying to himself.

5. **Finally, It's Important to Find an Advisor You Can Relate to on a Personal Level.** A good advisor will be a partner and ally for many years, guiding you on a long-distance financial journey. Sure, it's a professional relationship, but isn't money also a deeply personal subject for you, just as it is for me? It's tied up with our hopes and dreams, our desire to take care of the next generation, to have a charitable impact, to live an extraordinary life on our own terms. It helps if you can have these conversations with an advisor you connect with, trust, and like.

THE GRAND PRIZE

Much of this chapter has focused on the many obstacles we need to overcome in our quest for great financial advice: the conflicts of interest, the dissembling and deceit, the cynical and self-serving behavior. Isn't it extraordinary that it's so hard to find client-focused advisors with high-level skills who actually provide the service they *claim* to provide? No wonder so many people lose heart and decide to handle their finances on their own!

But let me tell you, there's a huge prize when you reach the finish line of this crazy obstacle course and find a truly great advisor. For many people, nothing has a more positive impact on their financial future than partnering with an intelligent guide who knows the territory and can show them proven ways to win in any environment. A world-class advisor will help you immeasurably from start to finish: defining your goals, keeping you on a steady path toward them—in particular, by helping you to weather market volatility—and massively increasing the probability that you'll actually achieve those goals.

Creative Planning, the registered investment advisory firm run by my co-author, Peter Mallouk, provides conflict-free investment advice that is also remarkably comprehensive. He's structured the company so that clients are advised by their own team, which includes experts on investing, mortgages, insurance, taxes, and even estate planning. The cost? Less than 1% annually (on average) for this entire team of experts.

This might sound like a service built exclusively for high-net-worth in-dividuals. But Peter and his team don't just service the ultrawealthy. At my request, he's created a special division to help clients who are early in their financial journey and have a minimum of $100,000 in assets.

I want to emphasize that I'm not pushing you to use Creative Planning, even though I'm the chief of investor psychology.

If you have someone else who can do a terrific job for you, I'm truly delighted. But I know how daunting it can be even to start the process of searching for great advice and figuring out who to trust. If you want a shortcut, you can start by asking Creative Planning for a free second opin-ion by visiting **www.getasecondopinion.com.** One of the firm's wealth managers can assess your situation and uncover whether or not your cur-rent advisor is operating in your best interests. If you want to go further and hire Creative Planning to serve as your fiduciary, we'd love to have you as part of the family.

Let me give you one example of why this holistic approach is so powerful. Many people own real estate investments outside of their more traditional investment portfolio but rarely are they accounted for when they're using a typical advisor. Imagine you own a number of properties. An advisor with the proper expertise will look at how to maximize your cash flow and might be able to help restructure the mortgages on those properties. The result? The ability to potentially invest in an additional property or two with no additional cash. In fact, your overall mortgage payments may be even lower than they were before! That's the benefit of truly sophisticated advice.

SEVEN KEY QUESTIONS TO ASK ANY ADVISOR

One way to make sure you hire the right advisor is to ask him or her sev-eral key questions that will help you to uncover any potential conflicts and concerns that you might miss otherwise. If you have an advisor already, it's equally important for you to get the answers to these questions. Here's what *I'd* want to know before placing my financial future in the hands of any advisor:

1. **Are You a Registered Investment Advisor?** If the answer is no, this advisor is a broker. Smile sweetly and say good-bye. If the answer is yes, he or she is required by law to be a fiduciary. But you still need to figure out if this fiduciary is wearing one hat or two.

2. **Are You (or Your Firm) Affiliated with a Broker-Dealer?** If the answer is yes, you're dealing with someone who can act as a broker and usually has an incentive to steer you to specific investments. One easy way to figure this out is to glance at the bottom of the advisor's website or business card and see if there's a sentence like this: "Securities offered through [advisor's company name], member FINRA and SIPC." This refers to the Financial Industry Regulatory Authority and the Securities Investor Protection Corporation, respectively. If you see these words, it means he or she can act as a broker. If so, run! Run for your life!

3. **Does Your Firm Offer Proprietary Mutual Funds or Separately Managed Accounts?** You want the answer to be an emphatic no. If the answer is yes, then watch your wallet like a hawk! It probably means they're looking to generate additional revenues by steering you into these products that are highly profitable for them (but probably not for you).

4. **Do You or Your Firm Receive Any Third-Party Compensation for Recommending Particular Investments?** This is the ultimate question you want answered. Why? Because you need to know that your advisor has no incentive to recommend products that will shower him or her with commissions, kickbacks, consulting fees, trips, or other goodies.

5. **What's Your Philosophy When It Comes to Investing?** This will help you to understand whether or not the advisor believes that he or she can beat the market by picking individual stocks or actively managed funds. Over time, that's a losing game unless the person is a total superstar like Ray Dalio or Warren Buffett. Between you and me, they're probably not.

6. **What Financial Planning Services Do You Offer Beyond Investment Strategy and Portfolio Management?** Investment help may be all you need, depending on your stage of life. But as you grow older and/or you become more wealthy with various holdings to manage, things often become more complex financially: for example, you may need to deal with saving for a child's college education, retirement planning, handling your vested stock options, or estate planning. Most advisors have limited capabilities once they venture beyond investing. As mentioned, most aren't legally allowed to offer tax advice due to their broker status. Ideally you want an advisor who can bring tools for tax efficiency in all aspects of your planning—from your investment planning to your business planning to your estate planning.

7. **Where Will My Money Be Held?** A fiduciary advisor should always use a third-party custodian to hold your funds. For example, Fidelity, Schwab, and TD Ameritrade all have custodial arms that will keep your money in a secure environment. **You then sign a limited power of attorney that gives the advisor the right to manage the money but never to make withdrawals.** The good news about this arrangement is that if you ever want to fire your advisor, you don't have to move your accounts. You can simply hire a new advisor who can take over managing your accounts without missing a beat. **This custodial system also protects you from the danger of getting fleeced by a con man like Bernie Madoff.**

MISSION ACCOMPLISHED!

We've covered an enormous amount of ground in section 1 of this book. As you'll recall, this section was designed as your rule book for financial success. Just think for a moment about some of the most important rules you've learned so far:

- You've learned the power of becoming a long-term investor who doesn't trade in and out of the market, who stays the course without getting shaken and stirred by corrections or crashes.

- You've learned that the vast majority of actively managed mutual funds overcharge for underperformance, which is why you're so much better off with inexpensive index funds that you can hold for many years.
- You've learned that excessive fees have a devastating effect, like termites eating away at the foundations of your financial future.
- And you've learned how to find an independent advisor who truly deserves—and will richly repay—your trust.

Now that you've completed the rule book, you're one of the few who actually understands how our financial system works. Now that you know the rules, you're ready to get in the game!

Section 2 of *Unshakeable* will give you a financial playbook that empowers you to put your personal action plan in place right now. In chapter 6, I'll share the Core Four principles that the world's best investors use in making investment decisions. In chapter 7, you'll learn how to "slay the bear" by constructing a diversified portfolio that protects you during market meltdowns. Then, in chapter 8, I'll show you how to "silence the enemy within"—letting you in on the most important secrets I've learned over 40 years on the psychology of wealth creation.

This playbook will give you the knowledge and the practical tools you need to achieve total financial freedom! Do you feel that *strength*, that *power*, coursing through your veins? Then turn the page—because it's time to design your playbook, take control, and *get in the game*. . . .

THE *UNSHAKEABLE* PLAYBOOK

CHAPTER 6

THE CORE FOUR

The Key Principles That Can Help Guide
Every Investment Decision You Make

Let's make it simple. Really simple.
—STEVE JOBS, cofounder of Apple

Anyone can get lucky and win the lottery. Anyone can pick a winning stock from time to time. But if you want to achieve *lasting* financial success, you need more than just the occasional lucky break. **What I've found over almost four decades of studying success is that the most successful people in any field aren't just lucky. They have a different set of beliefs. They have a different strategy. They do things differently than everyone else.**

I see this in every area of life, whether it's sustaining a happy and passionate marriage for more than a half century, losing weight and keeping it off for decades, or building a business worth billions.

The key is to recognize these consistently successful patterns and to model them, using them to guide the decisions you make in your own life. These patterns provide the playbook for your success.

When I embarked on my journey to find solutions that could help people financially, I studied the best of the best, ultimately interviewing more than 50 investment titans. I was determined to crack the code—to figure out what explains their stunning results. **Above all, I kept asking myself one question: What patterns do they have in common?**

As I soon realized, it was a remarkably difficult question to answer. The trouble is, all these brilliant investors have entirely different styles and approaches to making money. For example, Paul Tudor Jones is a trader who makes huge bets based on his macroeconomic view of the world. Warren Buffett makes long-term investments in public and private companies that possess a durable competitive advantage. Carl Icahn targets businesses that are underperforming, and then cajoles (or bludgeons) management to change its strategy in ways that can benefit shareholders. Clearly, there are many different paths to victory. Finding common denominators was quite a challenge!

But over the last seven years, I've done what I've always loved doing, which is to take complex subjects that seem overwhelming and break them down into a few core principles that people like you and me can actually utilize. So what did I discover? **I came to realize that there are four major principles that nearly all great investors use to guide them in making investment decisions. I call these the Core Four. These four patterns, which I'll explain in this chapter, can powerfully influence your ability to achieve financial freedom.**

Do you remember what I said earlier about complexity being the enemy of execution? Well, when I tell you about these four principles, you might respond by saying "How basic! How simple!" And you know what? You're right!

But it's not enough to *know* a principle. You have to *practice* it.

Execution is everything. I don't want to needlessly complicate matters so that you end up sitting on a mountain of rich information but don't know what to *do* with it. My goal isn't to dazzle you with elaborate arguments. It's to synthesize, simplify, and clarify so you feel empowered to take action now!

Together these principles provide us with an invaluable checklist. Whenever I'm speaking with my financial advisors about a potential investment, I want to know whether or not it meets the majority of these four criteria. If not, then I'm simply not interested.

Why am I so adamant about this? Because it's not enough to say "These are useful insights; I'll try to keep them in mind." **The best investors understand that these principles must be *obsessions*. They're so important that you need to internalize them, live by them, and make them the foundation of everything you do as an investor. In short, the Core Four should be at the very heart of your investment playbook.**

CORE PRINCIPLE 1: DON'T LOSE

The first question that every great investor asks constantly is this: "How can I avoid losing money?" This may sound counterintuitive. After all, most of us focus on exactly the opposite question: "How can I *make* money? How do I get the biggest possible return and hit the jackpot?"

But the best investors are obsessed with *avoiding losses*. Why? Because they understand a simple but profound fact: the more money you lose, the harder it is to get back to where you started.

I don't want you to feel like you're back in your high school math class! But it's worth pausing to clarify why losing money is such a disaster. Let's say you lose 50% of your money on a bad investment. How much will you need to earn to make yourself whole again? Most people would say 50%. But they'd be dead wrong.

Let's look at it. If you invested $100,000 and you lost 50%, you now have $50,000. If you then make a 50% return on that $50,000, you now have a total of $75,000. You're still down $25,000.

In reality, you'll need a *100%* gain just to recoup your losses and get back to your original $100,000. **And that could easily take you an entire decade.** This explains Warren Buffett's famous line about his first two rules of investing: "Rule number one: never lose money. Rule number two: never forget rule number one."

Other legendary investors are equally obsessed with avoiding losses. For example, my great friend Paul Tudor Jones told me, "The most important thing for me is that defense is 10 times more important than offense. . . . You have to be very focused on protecting the downside at all times."

But in practical terms, how can you actually avoid losing money? For a start, it's important to recognize that financial markets are wildly unpredictable. The talking heads on TV can pretend as much as they want that they know what's coming next. But don't fall for it! **The most successful investors recognize that none of us can consistently predict what the future holds. With that in mind, they always guard against the risk of unexpected events—and the risk that they themselves can be wrong, regardless of how smart they are.**

Take Ray Dalio. *Forbes* says he's produced $45 billion in profits for his investors—more than any other hedge fund manager in history. His net worth is estimated at $17.7 billion! I've met a lot of extraordinary people over the years, but I've never met anyone smarter than Ray. Even so, he told me that his entire investment approach is built on his awareness that the market will sometimes outsmart him, veering in a totally unexpected direction. He learned this lesson early in his career, thanks to what he described as "one of the most painful experiences" of his life.

In 1971, back when Ray was a young investor learning his trade, President Richard Nixon took the United States off the gold standard. In other words, dollars could no longer be directly converted into gold, which meant that the US currency was suddenly worth no more than the paper on which it was printed. Ray and everyone he knew in the investment community were certain that the stock market would plummet in response to this historic event. So what happened? Stocks skyrocketed! That's right. They did the *exact opposite* of what logic and reason told him and all the other experts to expect. "What I realized is nobody knows and nobody ever will," he says. "So I have to design an asset allocation that, even if I'm wrong, I'll still be okay."

That, my friend, is an insight that you and I should never forget: we have to design an asset allocation that ensures we'll "still be okay," even when we're wrong.

Asset allocation is simply a matter of establishing the right mix of different types of investments, diversifying among them in such a way that you reduce your risks and maximize your rewards.

> I don't look to jump over seven-foot bars: I look
> around for one-foot bars that I can step over.
> —WARREN BUFFETT

We'll discuss the ins and outs of asset allocation in much greater depth in the next chapter. But for now, it's important to remember this: we should always *expect the unexpected*. Does that mean we should hide away in fear because everything is so uncertain? Not at all. **It simply means that we should invest in ways that help to protect us from nasty surprises.**

As you and I both know, many investors get hurt by market bubbles because they start to act as if the future will bring nothing but sunshine. As a result, they throw caution to the wind. Long-time winners such as Bogle, Buffett, and Dalio know the future will be full of surprises, both pleasant and unpleasant. So they never forget about their downside risk, and they protect themselves by investing in different types of assets, some of which will rise while others fall.

I'm no economist or market seer! But it strikes me that this emphasis on avoiding loss is particularly relevant today, given that none of us can predict the effect of the radical economic policies we're seeing around the world. We're in uncharted territory. As Howard Marks told me in late 2016, "When you're in an uncertain world with high asset prices and low prospective returns, I think that should give you pause." At his $100 billion investment firm, Oaktree Capital Management, the mantra in recent years has been "Proceed with caution." He explains: "We are investing. We're fully invested. We're happy to be invested, but everything we're buying has an unusually high degree of caution."

How do I apply the "Do Not Lose" principle in my own life? I'm so obsessed with this idea of not losing that I now tell all my advisors, "Don't even bring me an investment idea unless you first tell me how we can protect against or minimize the downside."

CORE PRINCIPLE 2:
ASYMMETRIC RISK/REWARD

According to conventional wisdom, you need to take big risks to achieve big returns. But the best investors don't fall for this high-risk, high-return myth. **Instead, they hunt for investment opportunities that offer what they call asymmetric risk/reward: a fancy way of saying that the rewards should vastly outweigh the risks. In other words, these winning investors always seek to risk as little as possible to make as much as possible. That's the investor's equivalent of nirvana.**

I've seen this up close with Paul Tudor Jones, who uses a "five-to-one rule" to guide his investment decisions. "I'm risking one dollar in the expectation that I'll make five," he explained to me in the early days of our

©Jeff Stahler/Distributed by Universal Uclick for UFS via CartoonStock.com

coaching relationship. "What five-to-one does is allow you to have a hit rate of 20%. I can actually be a complete imbecile. I can be wrong 80% of the time, and I'm still not going to lose."

How is that possible? If Paul makes five investments, each for $1 million, and four in a row go to zero, then he's lost a total of $4 million. But if the fifth investment is a home run and makes $5 million, he's earned back his entire $5 million investment.

In reality, Paul's hit rate is a whole lot better than that! Imagine that only *two* of his five investments pan out as expected and go up fivefold. That means his original $5 million has just grown to $10 million. In other words, he's doubled his money despite, in this case, being wrong 60% of the time!

By applying his five-to-one rule, he sets himself up to win the game, despite some inevitable mistakes.

Now, let's be clear: five-to-one is Paul's *ideal* investment. He obviously can't find that ratio every time. In some cases, the ratio of three-to-one is his target. The larger point is, he's always looking for limited downside and huge upside.

Another friend of mine who's obsessed with asymmetric risk/reward is Sir Richard Branson, the founder of the Virgin Group. Richard, who oversees about four hundred companies, isn't just an inspired entrepreneur. He's also an adventurer with a dangerous passion for putting his life on the line, from hot-air ballooning around the globe, to setting the record for the fastest crossing of the English Channel in an amphibious vehicle! So he's the ultimate risk taker, right? Yes and no. It's true that he takes outlandish risks with his life. But when it comes to his finances, he's masterful at minimizing risk.

I'll give you a classic example: when he launched Virgin Atlantic Airways in 1984, Richard started with just five airplanes. He was challenging an entrenched Goliath, British Airways, in an infamously tough business. He once joked, "If you want to be a millionaire, start with a billion dollars and launch a new airline!" But Richard spent over a year negotiating an unbelievable deal that would allow him to return those planes if the business didn't pan out. That left him with minimal downside and limitless upside! "Superficially, I think it looks like entrepreneurs have a high tolerance for risk," he says. "But one of the most important phrases in my life is 'Protect the downside.'"

This pattern of thinking about asymmetric risk/reward cropped up again and again in my interviews with famous investors. Consider Carl Icahn, whose net worth is estimated at $17 billion and who was dubbed "Master of the Universe" on the cover of *Time* magazine. This is a guy whose compounded rate of return since 1968 was 31%, better even than Warren Buffett's 20%.[13] Carl earned a fortune by making huge investments in poorly run businesses and then threatening to take them over unless management agreed to mend its ways. This might seem like the world's riskiest game of high-stakes poker, with billions on the line.

But Carl never lost sight of the odds. "It appeared that we were risking a lot of money, but we weren't," he told me. "Everything is risk and reward. But you've got to understand what the risk is and also understand what the reward is. Most people saw much more risk than I did. But math doesn't lie, and they simply didn't understand it."

Are you starting to see a pattern here? These three multibillionaires—Paul Tudor Jones, Richard Branson, and Carl Icahn—have totally different approaches to making money. **Yet all three share the same obsession:** *how to reduce risks while maximizing returns.*

Now, forgive me if I'm wrong. But I'm guessing that you're not about to start a new airline or launch a hostile takeover of a company. So how can you apply this pattern of thinking in your own financial life?

One way to achieve asymmetric risk/reward is to invest in undervalued assets during times of mass pessimism and gloom. **As you'll learn in the next chapter, corrections and bear markets can be among the greatest financial gifts of your life.** Think back to the financial crisis of 2008–09. At the time, it felt like hell on earth. But if you had the right mind-set and your eyes were open, the opportunities were heavenly! You couldn't move without tripping over a bargain!

When the market hit rock bottom in March 2009, the future looked so bleak to most investors that you could snap up shares in blue-chip companies for pennies on the dollar. For example, Citigroup sank to a low of 97

---

13 According to *Kiplinger's Personal Finance*.

cents a share, down from a peak of $57! You could literally own a piece of the company for less than it cost you to take money out of an ATM. But here's the kicker: winter is always followed by springtime, and sometimes the seasons turn much quicker than you'd ever guess. This 97-cent stock shot to $5 within five months, giving investors a 500% return.

That's why "value" investors like Warren Buffett lick their chops during bear markets. The turmoil enables them to invest in beaten-up stocks at such low prices that the downside is limited and the upside is spectacular.

Buffett did just that in late 2008, investing in fallen giants such as Goldman Sachs and General Electric, which were selling at once-in-a-lifetime valuations. Better still, he structured these investments in ways that reduced his risk even further. For example, he invested $5 billion in a special class of "preferred" shares of Goldman Sachs, which guaranteed him a dividend of 10% a year while he waited for the stock price to recover!

Most people get so scared during crashes that they see *only* the downside. But Buffett made sure that it was almost impossible for him to lose.

In other words, it's all about asymmetric risk/reward!

Here is an example from my own personal investments. A window of opportunity opened up for me in the years following the 2008-09 financial crisis, when banks had decided to implement some of the most stringent lending requirements in years. At the time, many individuals had significant equity value in their homes but no way to access the funds. A refinancing, or re-fi, was out of the question. They were looking for a way to access short-term funds (typically one to two years or less) and were willing to post their home as collateral.

In short, I would lend them the funds they needed and became what is known as the "first trust deed holder" on their home. Back in 2009, a homeowner came to my team with a house valued at $2 million, and it was owned free and clear. He was requesting a $1 million loan (50% of the current appraised value of the property) and was willing to pay 10% interest for 12 months. Not bad in a world where I could invest in a 10-year Treasury note and currently earn only 1.8% a year. And since the Federal Reserve has already begun raising rates, that will put downward pressure on bond prices so my net return could be less (unless I am willing to hold all the way to maturity).

So what was my downside if I invested in the trust deed? If the borrower defaulted, the real estate market would have had to collapse by more than 50% for me to **not** get my money back. Even in the worst real estate downturn we've seen in over half a century (2008) this specific community did not see price decreases greater than 35%. So with a short one-year time horizon, this met the first of my criteria—how to increase my odds of not losing money!

Plus, look at the asymmetrical risk/reward: There was little risk of losing money, given that the real estate market could drop by 50% and I'd still break even; and a 10% annual return gave me plenty of upside in an environment of compressed returns. Based on these factors, I was confident that this investment offered an excellent balance of risk and reward.

Now you don't need to have a million dollars to do investments like this. Many borrowers were asking for $25,000 to $50,000 loans as well. But my point here is not that you should go hunting for first trust deeds. There are other risks associated with these types of investments that are important to understand. The point is, different opportunities will always present themselves, depending on the economic climate or market behavior.

CORE PRINCIPLE 3: TAX EFFICIENCY

As we discussed earlier, taxes can easily wipe out 30% or more of your investment returns if you're not careful. Yet mutual fund companies love to tout their *pretax* returns, obscuring the reality that **there's only one number that truly matters: the *net* amount that you actually get to keep.**

When people congratulate themselves on their investment returns without taking into account the impact of taxes (let alone fees), what they're really demonstrating is a gift for self-delusion! It's a bit like saying, "I was so good on my diet today," while conveniently forgetting that you scarfed down a couple of donuts, a double portion of French fries, and a hot-fudge sundae!

In investing, self-delusion is an expensive habit. So let's remove the blindfold and confront the unvarnished truth! If you're a high earner, you could currently be paying an ordinary income tax rate of 50% between federal and state taxes. If you sell an investment that you've owned for *less* than a year, your gains will be taxed at the same sky-high rate you pay on your ordinary income. Brutal, right?

By contrast, if you hold most investments for a year or more, you'll pay long-term capital gains tax when you sell. The current rate is 20%, which is *way* lower than the rate you pay on your ordinary income. Simply by being smart about your holding period, you're saving up to 30% on taxes.

But if you ignore the impact of taxes, you pay a heavy price. Let's say you own a mutual fund that earns 8% a year. After deducting fees of, say, 2% a year, you're left with 6%. If the fund trades frequently (as most funds do), then all those short-term gains will be taxed at your ordinary income rate.[14] So if you're a high earner in a state such as California or New York, your 6% annual return just got cut in half to a measly 3% *post-tax* return! At this rate, you'll double your money only every 24 years. But you also need to take into account the effect of inflation. If that comes in at 2% a year, your *real* return has just dropped from 3% to 1%. At this rate, you're likely to retire at the age of 120.

> I have enough money to retire and live comfortably for the rest
> of my life. The problem is, I have to die next week.
> —ANONYMOUS

Now can you see why it's so important to invest in a tax-efficient way? Believe me, all the billionaires I've ever met have one attribute in common: they and their advisors are really smart about taxes! **They know that it's not what they *earn* that counts. It's what they *keep*. That's *real* money, which they can spend, reinvest, or give away to improve the lives of others.**

In case you're wondering, there's nothing sordid or immoral about managing your finances in ways that lawfully reduce your tax burden. The authority most often quoted on this subject by legal scholars and the US Supreme Court is Federal Appeals Court Judge Billings Learned Hand. He famously stated in 1934: "Anyone may arrange his affairs so that his taxes

---

14 According to William Harding, an analyst with Morningstar, the average turnover ratio for managed domestic stock funds is 130%.

shall be as low as possible. . . . Nobody owes any public duty to pay more than the law demands."

When I met David Swensen, he pointed out that one of his biggest advantages in investing money for Yale is that it's a nonprofit institution and thus *exempt* from taxes. But what should the rest of us do? First, steer clear of actively managed funds, especially those that trade a lot. As David told me, one benefit of index funds is that they keep trading to a minimum, which means "your tax bill is going to be lower. This is huge. **One of the most serious problems in the mutual fund industry, which is full of serious problems, is that almost all mutual fund managers behave as if taxes don't matter. But taxes matter. Taxes matter a lot.**"

As he spoke, I could feel his deep concern, his determination to help people understand the significance of what he was saying. The enormous impact of taxes on your returns "speaks to the importance of taking advantage of every tax-advantaged investment opportunity that you can," David emphasized. "You should maximize your contributions if you've got a 401(k), or a 403(b) if you work for a nonprofit. You should take every opportunity to invest in a tax-deferred way."

It sounds so obvious, right? We all know that tax-advantaged vehicles such as 401(k)s, Roth IRAs, traditional IRAs, private placement life insurance (or PPLI, the "rich man's Roth"), and 529 plans (for college savings) can help us reach our goals quicker. You're probably taking advantage of some of these opportunities already. But if you're not *maximizing* your contributions, now is the time to do it!

If you want to learn more about this topic, *Money: Master the Game* covers it in depth in chapter 5.5: "Secrets of the Ultrawealthy (That You Can Use Too!)." Remember: one problem you'll encounter if you're using a broker is that they are not tax professionals, so they're not allowed legally to advise you on taxes. Even most registered investment advisors don't have a tax expert on their team to guide you in this area. That's why you ideally want to partner with a firm that has CPAs on staff, since they'll keep tax efficiency top of mind.

I've applied what David taught me. This tax-sensitive way of thinking permeates my approach to investing. Of course, I don't *start* with taxes. That would be a severe mistake. I always start with a focus on not losing money

and on getting asymmetric risk/reward. *Then*, before making any investment, I make a point of asking, "How tax efficient is this going to be? And is
there any way we could make it *more* tax efficient?"

One reason for this obsession is that I spent much of my life living in
California, where—after tax—I kept as little as 38 cents of every dollar I
earned. When you're taxed that heavily, it sensitizes you pretty quickly! I
learned to focus solely on what would be left *after* paying Uncle Sam his
due.

Whenever someone tells me about a financial opportunity that seems to
offer enticing returns, my response is always the same: "Is that *net*?" More
often than not, the person replies, "No, that's *gross*." But the pretax figure is
phony, whereas the *net* number doesn't lie. Your goal, and mine, is always to
maximize the net.

I'll give you a specific example: Creative Planning, where I serve as chief
of investor psychology, might recommend master limited partnerships
(MLPs) for certain client portfolios, when appropriate. As I soon learned,
these publicly traded partnerships offer an easy way to invest in energy infrastructure such as pipelines for oil, gasoline, and natural gas. I called my
friend T. Boone Pickens, who's made billions in the oil business, and asked,
"What do you think of MLPs right now?"

He explained that their price had tumbled because of a crash in energy
prices. In fact, from 2014 through early 2016, the price of oil had fallen
more than 70%. Many investors assumed that this drop was terrible news
for MLPs, since they provide infrastructure to clients in the energy business.
But MLPs—at least, the best of them—are much better protected than they
seem. That's because their clients typically sign long-term contracts with
fixed fees in return for the right to use this infrastructure. This provides a
reliable income stream year after year, enabling MLPs to pay out generous
royalty income to their partners.

As Boone explained, you're not really betting on oil and gas prices when
you invest in an MLP. As an owner of a pipeline, you're more like a toll col-
lector. Regardless of what happens to oil or gas prices, energy is going to
keep getting transported around the country, because it's the lifeblood of the
national economy. And, as an owner of the MLP, you'll keep collecting your
tolls like clockwork!

Meanwhile, the fact that the price of MLPs had nosedived was actually good news for investors. Why? Because this was an overreaction to the drop in the price of energy. Most investors were so fearful, that you could invest at a historically low valuation. Even some of the highest-quality MLPs had seen their prices fall 50%.

But the tollbooth was still working beautifully. An MLP that had sold previously for $100 paid an annual income royalty of $5 per share—that's 5% income per year on the investment. When the price dropped to $50, the MLP still paid out $5 per share of income. But this now amounted to a *10%* annual income return! That might not sound like a bonanza. But in this era of rock-bottom interest rates, it's a whole lot better than bonds that yield 2% or less. **Even better, you still had all of the upside if the price of the MLP recovered!**

So let's take a moment and see how MLPs stacked up against the criteria in our Core Four:

1. **Don't Lose.** The price of energy and MLPs had fallen so much that it was unlikely they'd fall significantly further. Experts like "the oil oracle" T. Boone Pickens also pointed out that energy production had shrunk massively because prices had cratered. That meant supplies were diminishing, and even with lesser demand, the prices would eventually have to rise. With all this on your side, the odds of losing money were greatly diminished.
2. **Asymmetric Risk/Reward.** As we've said, there was very little risk of loss. But there was a high probability that energy prices would eventually recover and that MLPs would return to favor. In the meantime, you'd be collecting 10% a year in annual income. Believe me, I'm happy to sit tight and collect my tolls!
3. **Tax Efficiency.** But here's the best part: the US government needs to promote domestic energy production and distribution, so it has given MLPs preferential tax treatment. **As a result, most of the income you receive is offset by depreciation, which means that roughly 80% of your income is tax free.** So if you make a 10% return, you're netting 8% annually. That's pretty nice, right? By contrast, if you *didn't* have this tax-preferential treatment, the income paid within the

year would be taxed at your ordinary income tax rate. A high income earner who pays 50% in taxes would net just 5%. In other words, by using the tax efficiency of an MLP, you net 8% instead of 5%. The difference: *60%* more money in your pocket. That's the power of tax efficiency.

As Peter will explain in the next chapter, MLPs aren't right for everyone—nor are we specifically recommending them for you. But it's the broader principle that I'm looking to illustrate here: by focusing on *after-tax returns*, you can put yourself on a much faster path to financial freedom.

Incidentally, it's worth pointing out that there's almost always an asset class or a country or a market that's getting clobbered, presenting you with equally enticing opportunities for asymmetrical risk/reward.

Finally, for good measure, being smart about your taxes also helps you to have a greater impact on the world. Instead of leaving the government to decide how to spend your money, you get to decide for yourself! My own life is infinitely richer because I'm able to support causes that excite and inspire me. I've been able to provide a quarter of a billion free meals so far, and I'm on my way to a target of one billion meals through my initiative with Feeding America. I'm also providing 250,000 people with fresh water every day in India, and I'm helping to save over 1,000 kids from sexual slavery through a partnership with Operation Underground Railroad.[15] These are just a few of the gifts I can share as a result of being tax efficient in my investments.

CORE PRINCIPLE 4: DIVERSIFICATION

The fourth and final principle in the Core Four is perhaps the most obvious and fundamental of all: diversification. In its essence, it's what almost everyone knows: don't put all your eggs in one basket. But there's a difference

---

15 Operation Underground Railroad (OUR) gathers the world's experts in extraction operations and in anti–child trafficking efforts to bring an end to child slavery. Its team consists of former CIA, Navy SEALs, and Special-Ops operatives that lead coordinated identification and extraction efforts.

between knowing what to do and actually *doing* what you know. As Princeton professor Burton Malkiel told me, there are four important ways to diversify effectively:

1. **Diversify Across Different Asset Classes.** Avoid putting all your money in real estate, stocks, bonds, or any single investment class.
2. **Diversify Within Asset Classes.** Don't put all your money in a favorite stock such as Apple, or a single MLP, or one piece of waterfront real estate that could be washed away in a storm.
3. **Diversify Across Markets, Countries, and Currencies Around the World.** We live in a global economy, so don't make the mistake of investing solely in your own country.
4. **Diversify Across Time.** You're never going to know the right time to buy anything. But if you keep adding to your investments systematically over months and years (in other words, dollar-cost averaging), you'll reduce your risk and increase your returns over time.

We are the last Dodos on the planet, so I've put
all of our eggs safely into this basket...

Every Hall of Fame investor I've ever interviewed is obsessed with the question of how best to diversify in order to maximize returns and minimize risks. Paul Tudor Jones told me, "I think the single most important thing you can do is diversify your portfolio." This message was echoed in my interviews with Jack Bogle, Warren Buffett, Howard Marks, David Swensen, JPMorgan's Mary Callahan Erdoes, and countless others.

The principle itself may be simple, but implementing it is another matter! That requires real expertise. This is such an important topic that we've devoted much of the next chapter to it. My co-author, Peter Mallouk—who guided his clients through the frightening crash of 2008–09—will explain how to build a customized asset allocation, diversifying among different types of investments such as stocks, bonds, real estate, and "alternatives." His mission: to help you construct a portfolio that will enable you to prosper in any environment.

This might sound like a big promise, but diversification does its job in the worst of seasons. Between 2000 and the end of 2009, US investors experienced what has become known as the "lost decade" because the S&P 500 was essentially flat despite its major swings. But smart investors look beyond just the largest US stocks. Burt Malkiel authored a *Wall Street Journal* article titled "'Buy and Hold' Is Still a Winner." In it he explained that if you were diversified among a basket of index funds—including US stocks, foreign stocks, and emerging-market stocks, bonds, and real estate—between the beginning of 2000 and the end of 2009, a $100,000 initial investment would have grown to $191,859. That's a 6.7% average annual return during the lost decade!

One reason why diversification is so critical is that it protects us from a natural human tendency to stick with whatever we feel we know. Once a person is comfortable with the idea that a particular approach works—or that he or she understands it well—it's tempting to become a one-trick pony! As a result, many people end up investing too heavily in one specific area. For example, they might stake everything on real estate because they grew up seeing it work like magic for their family; or they might be a gold bug; or they might bet too aggressively on a hot sector such as tech stocks.

The trouble is, everything is cyclical. And what's hot can now suddenly turn to ice. As Ray Dalio warned me, "It's almost certain that whatever [asset class] you're going to put your money in, there will come a day when you will lose 50%–70%." Can you imagine having most or all of your money in that one area and watching in horror as it goes up in flames? Diversification is your insurance policy against that nightmare. It decreases your risk and increases your return, yet it doesn't cost you extra. How's that for a winning combination?

Of course, there are many different ways of diversifying. I discuss this in detail in *Money: Master the Game*, laying out the exact asset allocations recommended by Ray and other financial gurus, such as Jack Bogle and David Swensen. For example, David told me how individual investors can diversify by owning low-cost index funds that invest in six "really important" asset classes: US stocks, international stocks, emerging-market stocks, real estate investment trusts (REITs), long-term US Treasuries, and Treasury inflation-protected securities (TIPS). He even shared the precise percentages that he would recommend allocating to each.

As for Ray Dalio, his unique approach to diversification does an extraordinary job of taming risk. I had the privilege of speaking right after my dear friend Ray at the Robin Hood Investors Conference in late 2016. The best investors in the business listened intently as Ray revealed one of the great secrets of his approach: "The holy grail of investing is to have 15 or more good—they don't have to be great—uncorrelated bets."

In other words, everything comes down to owning an array of attractive assets that don't move in tandem. That's how you ensure survival and success. In his case, this includes investments in stocks, bonds, gold, commodities, real estate, and other alternatives. **Ray emphasized that, by owning 15 uncorrelated investments, you can reduce your overall risk "by about 80%," and "you'll increase the return-to-risk ratio by a factor of five. So, your return is *five times greater* by reducing that risk."**

I'm not suggesting that there's a perfect, one-size-fits-all approach that you should necessarily follow. What I really want to convey is that all of the best investors regard diversification as a core component of long-term financial success. If you follow their example by diversifying broadly, you'll be prepared for anything, freeing you to face the future with calm confidence.

READY TO RUMBLE!

By now, you're already way ahead of the game. You belong to a tiny elite that understands these four all-important principles that the best investors use to guide their investment decisions. If you live by them, your odds of investment success will rise exponentially!

In the next chapter, we'll delve deeper into the nitty gritty of asset allocation. Peter Mallouk will explain the benefits of taking a customized approach that's tailored to your specific needs and circumstances. With his expert guidance, you'll learn to construct a diversified portfolio that enables you to weather any storm. Remember: we all know that winter is coming. We all know that bear markets are regular occurrences. Most investors live in fear of them. But you're about to discover how to make winter the best season of all—a season to *relish*!

So come with me, intrepid warrior! It's time to grab our weapons and *slay the bear*!

CHAPTER 7

SLAY THE BEAR

How to Navigate Crashes and Corrections to
Accelerate Your Financial Freedom

I learned that courage was not the absence of fear, but
the triumph over it. The brave man is not he who does
not feel afraid, but he who conquers that fear.
—NELSON MANDELA

THE PATH TO FEARLESSNESS

When I was 31 years old, I visited a doctor for my annual physical—a routine checkup that was required for me to renew my license as a helicopter pilot. In the days that followed, the doctor left several messages asking me to call him. I was running around like crazy and didn't have time to speak with him. Then, one evening, I got home after midnight and found a note that my assistant had taped to my bedroom door: "You *must* call the doctor. He says it's an emergency."

You can imagine how my mind began to race. I was extremely disciplined about my health, and I'd never felt fitter. So what could possibly be wrong? The mind tends to go crazy in times like this. I began to wonder: "I travel a lot, so maybe it's related to the radiation on airplanes. Could I have cancer? Could I be dying?" Surely not.

I pulled myself together and managed to get some sleep. But when I woke up the next morning, I was filled with fear and dread. I phoned the doctor, and he told me: "You need surgery. You have a tumor in your brain."

I was stunned. "What are you talking about? How could you know that?" The doctor, a combative guy with no bedside manner, said he'd done some extra blood tests because he believed that I had an enormous amount of growth hormone in my body. It didn't take a genius to figure that out, given that I'm six foot seven and had shot up 10 inches in a single year when I was 17. But he was convinced that this explosive growth was the result of a tumor in the pituitary gland at the base of my brain. He wanted me to come in immediately and have the tumor cut out.

I was scheduled to fly to the South of France the next day to teach a Date with Destiny seminar. But I was now supposed to drop everything and undergo emergency surgery? So much for destiny! I went ahead and taught the seminar anyway, and then traveled to Italy, where I stayed in a beautiful fishing village called Portofino. But it was there that I started freaking out. I felt like a different human being, getting angry and frustrated at little things. What was *wrong* with me?

Growing up, I'd lived in a world with no certainty. When my mom was on drugs and angry, she'd sometimes lose control over little things. If she thought I was lying about something she might pour soap in my mouth until I threw up—or smash my head against a wall. Since then, I'd spent a lifetime training and conditioning myself to find certainty *in an uncertain world*. But I'd allowed this doctor's comments to suddenly plunge me into the deepest level of uncertainty. Out of nowhere, my world had been turned upside down, and the life I'd built was crumbling. After all, how can you be certain about *anything* when you're uncertain about the most basic question: "Am I going to live or die?"

Sitting in a church in Portofino, I prayed for dear life. Then I decided to go home and deal head-on with this situation. The next few days were surreal. I remember coming out of the MRI machine and seeing the grim look on the lab technician's face. He said there was definitely a mass there, but he wouldn't give me any details until the doctor had interpreted the scan. The doctor was busy, so I had to wait another 24 hours. Now I knew for sure that I had a problem, but I still had no idea whether or not it was fatal.

Finally, the doctor met with me to explain my test results. The scan confirmed that I had a tumor, but also showed that it had miraculously shrunk by 60% over the years. I had no negative symptoms, and I hadn't grown since I was 17. So why did I need surgery? The doctor warned me that excessive growth hormone could trigger an array of health problems, including heart failure. "You're in denial," he said. "We have to operate immediately."

But what about the side effects? Beyond the danger of dying under the knife, the biggest risk was that the operation would damage my endocrine system, so that I'd never again have the same level of energy. This was a price I wasn't prepared to pay. My mission of helping people to transform their lives requires tremendous energy and passion. I kept wondering, what if the surgery left me unable to do my life's work? To give you an idea, my average weekend event today has 10,000 people in attendance and goes for 50 hours over 4 days. In today's world, most people won't sit through a 3-hour movie that someone spent $300 million to make! So without enormous energy, there is no way I could deliver an experience where people from 40 different countries are not only totally engaged, but feel like they've completely transformed their lives.

The doctor was furious with me: "Without surgery, you can't be sure that you'll live." I wanted a second opinion, but he refused to recommend another doctor.

Through friends, I eventually found my way to a legendary endocrinologist in Boston. He scanned my brain again and then sat me down to review the results. He was a wonderful man, full of compassion, and his attitude was entirely different. He said I didn't need surgery; the risks were too great. Instead, he suggested that I fly to Switzerland twice a year for an injection of an experimental drug that hadn't yet been approved in the United States. He was certain this drug would stop my tumor from expanding and prevent the growth hormone from causing dangerous heart problems.

When I told him about the doctor who wanted to cut into my brain, he laughed and said: "The butcher wants to butcher, the baker wants to bake, the surgeon wants to cut, and I want to drug you!" It was true. We all like to do whatever we know best in order to achieve certainty. The problem was, this drug was also likely to have a profound effect on my energy level. The endocrinologist could see why this troubled me so deeply. "You're like Samson," he said. "You're afraid that you'll lose your power if we cut your hair!"

I asked him what would happen if I did nothing—no surgery, no drugs. "I don't know," he replied. "Nobody knows."

"So why should I take this drug?"

"If you *don't* take it," he said, "you can't be certain that you'll survive."

But by now, I no longer felt *un*certain. There was no evidence that my health had deteriorated in 14 years. So why should I roll the dice by having high-risk surgery or being injected with an experimental drug? I went to see a series of additional doctors until I found one who told me, "Tony, it's true, you have an enormous amount of growth hormone in your bloodstream. But it hasn't had any negative side effects. In fact, it may be helping your body to recover more quickly. I know body builders who would have to spend $1,200 a month to get what you're getting for free!"

In the end, I decided to do nothing more than get myself tested every few years to see if my condition had worsened. I didn't realize it then, but I'd just dodged a lethal bullet: the US Food and Drug Administration later outlawed that drug, based on studies showing that it caused cancer. Despite his best intentions, my big-hearted endocrinologist's flawed advice could have ruined my life.

And you know what? Twenty-five years later, I *still* have that tumor. In the meantime, I've had an amazing life, and I've been blessed with the opportunity to help millions of people along the way. This was possible only because I made myself unshakeable in the face of uncertainty. If I'd overreacted or followed unquestioningly the advice of either doctor without considering all of my options, I'd be missing a part of my brain, or I'd have cancer, or perhaps I'd be dead. If I'd relied on *them* for my certainty, it would have been catastrophic. Instead, I found certainty within myself, even though nothing in my external circumstances had changed.

Could I die tomorrow because of my brain tumor? Yes. I could also get hit by a truck as I cross the street. Still, I don't live in fear of what's going to happen. I shut that off. **You can be unshakeable, too, but this is a gift that only *you* can give yourself.** When it comes to the areas of your life that matter most—your family, your faith, your health, your finances—you can't rely on anybody else to tell you what to do. It's great to get coaching from experts in the field, but you can't outsource the final decision. You can't give another person control over *your* destiny, no matter how sincere or skilled he or she may be.

Why am I telling you this story of life and death in a book about money and investing? Because it's important to understand that there's *never* absolute certainty in life. **If you want to be certain that you'll never lose money in the financial markets, you can keep your savings in cash—but then you'll never stand a chance of achieving financial freedom. As Warren Buffett says, "We pay a high price for certainty."**

Even so, many people avoid financial risk because uncertainty terrifies them. In 2008 the US stock market plunged by 37% (and it crashed more than 50% from peak to trough). Five years later, a survey by Prudential Financial found that 44% of Americans *still* vowed never to invest in stocks again because they were so scarred by their memories of the financial crisis. In 2015 another survey discovered that nearly 60% of millennials distrusted financial markets, having lived through the crash of 2008–09. According to State Street Corporation's Center for Applied Research, many millennials keep 40% of their savings in cash!

I'm heartbroken to see that so many millennials aren't investing. **Because let me tell you: if you live in fear, you've lost the game before it even begins. How can you achieve anything if you're too scared to take a risk?** As Shakespeare wrote four centuries ago, "Cowards die many times before their deaths; the valiant never taste of death but once."

Let me be clear with you: I'm not suggesting that you take reckless risks! When it came to my health, I met with multiple experts, explored all the options, and let the facts guide me—not somebody else's emotions or professional biases. I then made an informed decision for myself that put the probabilities on my side. This process allowed me to move from uncertainty to unshakeable certainty.

It's the same with investing. **You can never *know* what the stock market will do. But that uncertainty isn't an excuse for inaction.** You can take control by educating yourself, studying the market's long-term patterns, modeling the best investors, and making rational decisions based on an understanding of what's worked for them over decades. As Warren Buffett says, **"Risk comes from not knowing what you're doing."**

There's one thing we *do* know for sure: there will be market crashes in the future, just as there were in the past. But does it make sense to be paralyzed with fear merely because there's a risk of getting hurt? Believe me, it wasn't easy to find out that I had a brain tumor. But I've flourished for the past 25 years because I learned to live fearlessly. Does being fearless mean having *no* fear? No! It means fearing *less*. When the next bear market comes and others are overwhelmed with fear, I want you to have the knowledge and fortitude to fear *less*. This fearlessness in the face of uncertainty will bring you tremendous financial rewards.

In fact, while others live in terror of bear markets, you'll discover in this chapter that they are the single greatest opportunity for building wealth in your lifetime. Why? Because that's when everything goes on sale! Imagine longing to own a Ferrari and discovering that you can buy one for half price. Would you be downhearted? No way! Yet when the stock market goes on sale, most people react as if it's a disaster! You need to understand that bear markets are here to serve you. If you keep your cool, they will actually accelerate your journey to financial freedom. If you find internal certainty, you'll actually be *excited* when the market crashes.

I'm now going to pass the baton to my friend and partner Peter Mallouk, who will explain how he and his firm, Creative Planning, navigated through the last great bear market back in 2008–09. Peter doesn't like to boast about his phenomenal results. But let me tell you, he handled the crisis so masterfully that his firm's assets under management rose from $500 million in 2008 to more than $1.8 billion in 2010, with hardly any advertising or marketing—and he now oversees $35 billion and counting. What's more, Creative Planning is the only company ever named by *Barron's* as the top independent financial advisor three years in a row. Then in 2017, Creative Planning topped the charts again as the number-one wealth management firm in America (by *Barron's*).

Peter will show you how to prepare for and profit from a bear market. As he'll explain, it all starts with building a diversified portfolio that can prosper through thick and thin. He'll give you invaluable advice on the art of asset allocation. Armed with this knowledge, you'll have nothing to fear from market mayhem. While others flee, you'll stand your ground and slay the bear!

PREPARE FOR THE BEAR

By Peter Mallouk

A simple rule dictates my buying: be fearful when others
are greedy, and be greedy when others are fearful.
And most certainly, fear is now widespread.
—WARREN BUFFETT IN OCTOBER 2008, explaining
why he was buying stocks as the market crashed

The Eye of the Storm

On September 29, 2008, the Dow Jones Industrial Average plunged 777 points. It was the biggest one-day drop ever, obliterating $1.2 trillion in wealth. That same day, the VIX index, a barometer of fear among investors, hit its highest level in history. By March 5, 2009, the market had tumbled more than 50%, devastated by the worst financial crisis since the Great Depression.

This was the perfect storm. Banks collapsed. High-flying funds blew up and crashed to the ground. Some of Wall Street's most renowned investors saw their reputations shattered. Yet I look back on that tumultuous time as one of the highlights of my career—a time when my wealth management firm, Creative

Planning, guided its clients to safety, positioning them so they not only survived the crash but also benefited enormously from the rebound that followed.

Tony has asked me to share this story with you because it embodies a central lesson of this book: bear markets are either the best of times or the worst of times, depending on *your* decisions. **If you make the wrong decisions, as most people did in 2008 and 2009, it can be financially catastrophic, setting you back years or even decades. But if you make the right decisions, as my firm and its clients did, then you have nothing to fear.** You'll even learn to welcome bear markets because of the unparalleled opportunities they create for coolheaded bargain hunters.

How did our ship survive the storm while many others sank to the bottom of the sea? First of all, we were in a better ship! Long before the bear market occurred, we prepared for it in the knowledge that blue skies never last, that hurricanes are inevitable. None of us knows *when* a bear market will come, how *bad* it will be, or how *long* it will last. But as you learned in chapter 2, they've occurred, on average, every 3 years over the last 115 years. That's not a reason to hide in terror. It's a reason to ensure that your vessel is safe and seaworthy, regardless of the conditions.

As we'll discuss in detail in this chapter, there are two primary ways to prepare for market turmoil. First, you need the right asset allocation—a fancy term for the proportion of your portfolio that's invested in different types of assets, including stocks, bonds, real estate, and alternative investments. Second, you need to be positioned conservatively enough (with some income set aside for a very rainy day), so that you won't be forced to sell while stocks are down. It's the financial equivalent of making sure you're equipped with safety harnesses, life vests, and sufficient food before heading out to sea. **As I see it, 90% of surviving a bear market comes down to preparation.**

What's the other 10%? That's all about how you react emotionally in the midst of the storm. Many people believe they'll have ice in their veins. But as you may have experienced yourself, it's psychologically intense when the market is melting down and panic is in the air. That's one reason why having a battle-hardened financial advisor can be helpful. It provides an emotional ballast, helping you remain calm so you don't waver at the worst moment and jump overboard!

One advantage our clients had is that we'd gone to great lengths to educate them in advance, so they wouldn't be in shock when a crash occurred. They understood *why* they owned what they owned, and they knew how these investments were likely to perform in a crash. It's like being warned by your doctor that a medication might make you dizzy and nauseous; you're not thrilled when this risk becomes a reality, but you'll cope much better than if it were a total surprise!

Even so, some clients needed a lot of reassurance. "Shouldn't we get out of stocks now and go to cash?" they'd ask. "Doesn't this crash feel different?" This reminded me of Sir John Templeton's famous remark: "The four most expensive words in investing are 'This time it's different.'" In the midst of a market meltdown, people *always* think this time is different! Battered by all the bad news in the media each day, they begin to wonder if the market will ever recover—or if something has fundamentally broken that can't be fixed.

I kept reminding my clients that every bear market in US history has eventually become a bull market, regardless of how bleak the news seemed at the time. Just think of the many calamities and crises of the twentieth century: the 1918 flu pandemic, which killed as many as 50 million people

James never left his bed, seeing nothing but danger in the financial world.

worldwide; the Wall Street crash of 1929, followed by the Great Depression; two world wars; many other bloody conflicts, from Vietnam to the Gulf; the Watergate scandal that brought about the resignation of President Nixon; plus countless economic recessions and market panics. So how did the stock market fare in that chaos-filled century? **The Dow Jones Industrial Average rose inexorably from 66 to 11,497.**

Here's what you have to remember, based on more than a century of history: the short-term outlook may look dire, but the stock market *always* rebounds. Why would you ever bet against this long-term pattern of resilience and recovery? This historical perspective gives me unshakeable peace of mind, and I hope it will help you to keep your eyes on the prize, regardless of the corrections and crashes we encounter in the years and decades to come.

The best investors know that the gloom *never* lasts. For example, Templeton made his first fortune by investing in dirt-cheap US stocks during the dark days of World War II. He later explained that he liked to invest at "the point of maximum pessimism," when bargains were everywhere. Likewise, Warren Buffett invested aggressively in 1974 when markets were slammed by the Arab oil embargo and Watergate. While others were filled with despair, he was exuberantly bullish, telling *Forbes*: "Now is the time to invest and get rich."

Psychologically, it's not easy to buy when pessimism is rampant. But the rewards often come spectacularly fast. The S&P 500 hit rock bottom in October 1974 and then jumped 38% in the next 12 months. In August 1982, with inflation out of control and interest rates at almost 20%, the S&P 500 bottomed out again—and then soared 59% in 12 months. Can you imagine how investors felt if they'd panicked and sold during those bear markets? They not only made the disastrous mistake of locking in their losses but missed out on those massive gains as the market revived. That's the price of fear.

When the bear struck again in 2008, I was determined to make the most of this opportunity. I had no idea when the market would recover, but I was certain it *would* recover. At the height of the crisis, I wrote to our clients: "There is simply no precedent, ever in history, of the market staying at a valuation level this low. . . . There are only two potential outcomes: the end of America as we know it or a recovery. Every time investors have bet on the former, they have lost."

Throughout the crash, we continued to invest heavily in the stock market on behalf of our clients. We took profits from strong asset classes such as bonds and invested the proceeds in weak asset classes such as US small-cap and large-cap stocks, international stocks, and emerging-market stocks. Instead of betting on individual companies, we bought index funds, which gave us instant diversification (at a low cost) across these massively undervalued markets.

How did this work out? Well, after bottoming out in March 2009, the S&P 500 shot up by 69.5% in just 12 months. **Over 5 years, the index rose 178%, vindicating our belief that bear markets are the ultimate gift for opportunistic investors with a long-term perspective. As I write this, the market has risen 266% since the 2009 low.**

As you can imagine, our clients were ecstatic. I'm proud to say that our clients held firm during the crash and hardly any abandoned ship. As a result, they profited handsomely from the recovery. Only two clients that left stand out in my memory. One of the two who abandoned our strategy was a new client who'd come to us shortly before the crisis with a portfolio loaded with real estate. We helped him diversify, which saved him a fortune when the property market crashed. But he couldn't cope with the volatility of the stock market. He panicked and put all his money in cash.

I called him a year later to see how he was doing. By then, the market had rallied dramatically. But he was still waiting on the sidelines, too nervous to invest. For all I know, he's *still* waiting and has missed the entire bull market of the last seven years. As Tony mentioned, you pay a high price for certainty.

The other client who left Creative Planning during that time was overwhelmed by the barrage of alarmist news in the media. He'd hear a pundit claiming that the market would fall 90%, or the dollar would collapse, or the United States would declare bankruptcy, and these warnings terrified him. To make matters worse, his daughter fed these fears. She worked at Goldman Sachs, where she had no shortage of brilliant colleagues. But one colleague convinced her that the financial system would collapse and that gold was the only safe haven. Her father listened, cashed out of stocks at the worst moment, and lost a fortune in gold. When I spoke with him months later, stocks were skyrocketing, but he feared it was too late for him to get back in. He was utterly dejected.

It saddens me to say this, but these two former clients have both suffered permanent financial damage because of rash decisions they made during the bear market. The reason? Their emotions got the better of them. In the next chapter, we'll look at how to avoid some of the most common psychological mistakes that trip up investors. **But first, let's focus on an equally critical subject: how to prepare for the *next* bear market by constructing a diversified portfolio that reduces your risks and enhances your returns.** This will help you to generate increasing wealth in any environment *and* allow you to sleep soundly at night!

The Ingredients of Success

Harry Markowitz, the Nobel Prize–winning economist, famously declared that diversification is the "only free lunch" in investing. If so, what are the ingredients? We'll run through them quickly here, looking at stocks, bonds, and alternative investments. Then we'll discuss how to mix these together to create a well-diversified portfolio. But before we get to that, it's worth clarifying *why* a portfolio should include multiple asset classes.

Let's start with a simple thought experiment. Imagine that I have a bunch of guests in my house. I offer them $1 each to walk across the street. As it happens, I live on a quiet suburban road with little traffic. So my offer feels like free money. But let's say I repeat the offer, and this time I give them two choices: either they can cross my street for $1, or they can cross a four-lane highway for $1. Nobody will take me up on this offer to cross the highway. But what if I offer $1,000 or $10,000? At some point, I'll arrive at a figure that entices *someone* to cross that highway!

What I've just illustrated is the relationship between risk and reward. There's a risk of injury in both scenarios—and, as that risk increases, the reward must rise in order for this to be perceived as a fair deal. **The additional reward you receive for taking that additional risk is called a risk premium.** When experts determine your asset allocation, they evaluate the risk premium for each asset. The riskier an asset seems to be, the greater the rate of return an investor will demand.

As a financial advisor, I construct a client's portfolio by combining asset classes, each with different risk characteristics and different rates of return. **The goal? To balance the *return* you need to achieve with the *risk* you're comfortable taking.** The beauty of diversification is that it can allow you to achieve a higher return without exposing yourself to greater risk. How come? Because different asset classes don't usually move in tandem. In 2008 the S&P 500 fell 38%, whereas investment grade bonds rose 5.24%.[16] If you owned stocks *and* bonds, you took less risk—and achieved better returns—than if you owned only stocks.

Now let's look at the major asset classes we can combine to help you reach the promised land!

Stocks

When you buy a stock, you're not buying a lottery ticket. You're becoming a part owner of a real operating business. The value of your shares will rise or fall based on the company's perceived fortunes. Many stocks also pay dividends, which are quarterly distributions of profits back to the shareholders. By investing in a stock, you're making the shift from being a consumer to being an owner. If you buy an iPhone, you're a consumer of Apple products; if you buy Apple stock, you're an owner of the company—and are entitled to a percentage of its future earnings.

What can you expect to earn as an investor in stocks? It's impossible to predict, but we can use the past as a (very) rough guide. *Historically, the stock market has returned an average of 9% to 10% a year over more than a century.* But these figures are deceptive because stocks can be wildly volatile along the way. It's not unusual for the market to fall 20% to 50% every few years. **On average, the market is down about one in every four years.** You need to recognize this reality so you won't be shocked when stocks tumble—and so you'll avoid excessive risks. **At the same time, it's useful to recognize that the market has made money three out of every four years.**

In the short term, the stock market is entirely unpredictable, despite the claims of "experts" who pretend to know what's going on! In January 2016,

16 2008 performance of Bloomberg Barclays US Aggregate Bond Index.

the S&P 500 suddenly sank 11%; then it made a U-turn and rose nearly as rapidly.

Why? Howard Marks, one of America's most respected investors, candidly told Tony, "There was no good reason for the decline. Equally, there was no good reason for the recovery."

But in the long run, nothing reflects economic expansion better than the stock market. **Over time the economy and the population grow, and workers become more productive. This rising economic tide makes businesses more profitable, which drives up stock prices.** That explains why the market soared over the course of the twentieth century, despite all those wars, crashes, and crises. Now do you see why it pays to invest in the stock market for the long term?

Nobody understands this better than Warren Buffett. In October 2008 he wrote an article for the *New York Times* encouraging people to buy US stocks while they were on sale, even though the financial world was "a mess" and the "headlines will continue to be scary." He wrote: "Think back to the early days of World War II, when things were going badly for the United States in Europe and the Pacific. The market hit bottom in April 1942, well before Allied fortunes turned. Again, in the early 1980s, the time to buy stocks was when inflation raged and the economy was in the tank. **In short, bad news is an investor's best friend**. It lets you buy a slice of America's future at a marked-down price. Over the long term, the stock market news will be good."

I suggest you commit that line to memory: *"Over the long term, the stock market news will be good."* **If you truly understand this, it will help you to be patient, unshakeable, and ultimately rich.**

So where do stocks fit within your portfolio? If you believe that the economy and businesses will be doing better 10 years from now, it makes sense to allocate a good portion of your investments to the stock market. **Over a 10-year period, the market *almost* always rises. Still, there are no guarantees.** A study by asset management company BlackRock showed that the market averaged -1% per year from 1929 to 1938. The good news? BlackRock noted that this 10-year losing streak was followed by two consecutive 10-year periods of robust gains as the market resumed its upward trajectory.

Of course, the challenge is to stay in the market long enough to enjoy these gains. The last thing you want is to be a forced seller during a prolonged bear market. How do you avoid that fate? For a start, don't live beyond your means or saddle yourself with too much debt—both reliable ways to put yourself in a vulnerable position. As much as possible, try to keep a financial cushion, so you'll never have to raise cash by selling stocks when the market is crashing. One way to build and maintain that cushion is to invest in bonds.

Bonds

When you buy a bond, you're making a loan to a government, a company, or some other entity. The financial services industry loves to make this stuff seem complex, but it's pretty simple. Bonds are loans. When you lend money to the federal government, it's called a *Treasury* bond. When you lend money to a city, state, or county, it's a *municipal* bond. When you lend money to a company such as Microsoft, it's a *corporate* bond. And when you lend money to a less dependable company, it's called a *high-yield* bond or a *junk* bond. Voilà! You've now completed Bonds 101.

How much can you earn as a money lender? It depends. Loaning money to the US government won't earn you much because there's little risk that it'll renege on its debts. Loaning money to the government of Venezuela (where inflation may hit 700% this year) is way riskier, so the interest rates need to be much higher. Again, it's all a trade-off between risk and reward. The US government is asking you to cross a traffic-free rural road on a sunny day; the Venezuelan government is asking you to cross a busy highway on a stormy night while wearing a blindfold.

The odds that a company will go bust and fail to repay its bondholders are higher than the odds that the US government will default on its loans. So the company has to pay a higher rate of return. Similarly, a young tech firm that wants to borrow money must pay a higher rate than a blue-chip giant such as Microsoft. Rating agencies like Moody's use terms such as "Aaa" and "Baa3" to grade these credit risks.

The other critical factor is the duration of the loan. The US government will currently pay you about 1.8% a year for a 10-year loan. If you lend the government that money for 30 years, you'll earn about 2.4% a year. There's a simple reason why you receive a higher rate for lending the money over a longer period: it's riskier.

Why do people want to own bonds? For a start, they're much safer than stocks. That's because the borrower is legally required to repay you. If you hold a bond to maturity, you'll receive all of your original loan back, plus the interest payments—unless the bond issuer goes bankrupt. As an asset class, bonds deliver positive calendar-year returns approximately 85% of the time.

So where do bonds make sense in your portfolio? Conservative investors who are retired or can't tolerate the volatility of stocks might choose to invest a large percentage of their assets in bonds. Less conservative investors might put a smaller portion of their assets in high-quality bonds to meet any financial needs that could arise over the next two to seven years. More aggressive investors might keep a portion of their money in bonds to provide them with "dry powder" that they can use when the stock market goes on sale. **This is exactly what Creative Planning did during the financial crisis: we sold some of our clients' bonds and invested the proceeds in the stock market, snapping up once-in-a-lifetime bargains.**

There's just one problem: it's hard to be enthusiastic about bonds in today's weird economic environment. Yields are abysmally low, so you earn a paltry return for the risk you're taking. It seems particularly unappealing to invest in US Treasuries, which recently offered their lowest yields ever. Overseas, the situation gets even wilder: the Italian government recently sold a 50-year bond with a 2.8% interest rate. That's right! If you loan your money for a *half century*, you might be "lucky" enough to make 2.8% a year—*if* this economically vulnerable country doesn't run into trouble. It's one of the worst bets I've ever seen.

The challenge is that you earn *nothing* these days if you keep your money in cash. In fact, after inflation, you're losing money by holding cash. At least bonds provide *some* income. As I see it, bonds are now the cleanest dirty clothing in the laundry pile.

Alternative Investments

Any investments other than stocks, bonds, and cash are defined as alternatives. That includes exotic assets such as your Pablo Picasso collection, your cellar full of rare wines, the vintage cars in your air-conditioned garage, your priceless jewels, and your 100,000-acre ranch. But we'll focus here on a few of the most popular alternatives, which are likely to be relevant to a broader audience.

First, a word of warning: many alternatives are illiquid (in other words, hard to sell), tax inefficient, and laden with high expenses. That said, they have two attractive attributes: they can (sometimes) generate superior returns; and they may be uncorrelated to the stock and bond markets, which means they can help to diversify your portfolio and reduce overall risk. For example, if the stock market drops 50%, you don't suffer a 50% drop in your net worth, because all your eggs aren't in one basket. Any challenge you face is much smaller.

Let's look at five alternatives, starting with three that I like, followed by two that I don't:

- **Real Estate Investment Trusts.** I'm sure you know people who've done well by investing directly in residential property. But most of us can't afford to diversify by owning a slew of houses or apartments. That's one reason why I like to invest in publicly traded real estate investment trusts (REITs). They provide a no-hassle, low-cost way to diversify broadly, both geographically and across different types of property. For example, you can own a small slice of a REIT that invests in assets such as apartment buildings, office towers, senior housing facilities, medical offices, or shopping malls. You get to benefit from any appreciation in the price of the underlying property, while also receiving a healthy stream of current income.

- **Private Equity Funds.** Private equity firms use pooled money to buy all or part of an operating company. They can then add value by, say, restructuring the business, cutting costs, and minimizing taxes. Ultimately, they attempt to resell the company for a much higher price. The upside: a private equity fund that's run with true expertise can make outsized profits while also adding diversification to your portfolio by operating in the private market. The downside: these funds are illiquid, risky, and charge high fees. At Creative Planning, we're able to leverage our relationships, and $35 billion in assets, in order to gain access to funds managed by one of the country's top-10 private equity companies. Their minimum investment is usually $10 million, but our clients can invest with a minimum of $1 million. As you can see, this isn't for everyone, but the best funds may well earn their high fees.

- **Master Limited Partnerships.** I'm a big fan of MLPs, which are publicly traded partnerships that typically invest in energy infrastructure, including oil and gas pipelines. What's the appeal? As Tony mentioned in the last chapter, we sometimes recommend MLPs because they pay out a lot of income in a tax-efficient way. They don't make sense for many investors (especially if you're young or have your money in an IRA), but they can be great for an investor who is over 50 and has a large, taxable account.

- **Gold.** Some people have an almost religious belief that gold is the perfect hedge against economic chaos. They argue that it'll be the one true currency if the economy falls apart, inflation soars, or the dollar collapses. My view? Gold produces no income and is not a critical resource. As Warren Buffett said once, "Gold gets dug out of the ground in Africa, or someplace. Then we melt it down, dig another hole, bury it again, and pay people to stand around guarding it. It has no utility. Anyone watching from Mars would be scratching their head." Even so, gold prices soar occasionally, and everyone piles in! Every time—without exception—the price has ultimately collapsed. Historically, stocks, bonds, energy commodities, and real estate have outperformed gold. So count me out.

- **Hedge Funds.** At Creative Planning, we have no place for hedge funds in our portfolios. Why not? A few of these private partnerships have performed brilliantly over many years, but it's a minuscule minority—and the very best of them tend to be closed to new investors. The problem is, hedge funds start with a huge disadvantage in every major category: fees, taxes, risk management, transparency, and liquidity. Most charge 2% a year, no matter what, plus 20% of their investors' profits. What do you get in return? Well, from 2009 to 2015, the average hedge fund lagged the S&P 500 for 6 years in a row. In 2014 the nation's largest pension fund, CalPERS (the California Public Employees' Retirement System), abandoned hedge funds entirely. As I see it, hedge funds are handmade for suckers or for speculators looking to roll the dice on a big bet. They'll make *someone* rich, but it ain't likely to be you or me.

A CUSTOMIZED APPROACH TO
ASSET ALLOCATION

Now you know what ingredients you can use, but how should you combine them to create the perfect meal? The truth is, there's no single method that's right for everyone. Yet many advisors use a cookie-cutter approach to asset allocation, ignoring critical differences in their clients' needs. That's like serving steak to a vegetarian or kale salad to a carnivore.

One common—but misguided—approach involves using a person's age to determine the percentage of bonds in his or her portfolio. For example, if you're 55, you'd have 55% of your assets allocated to bonds. To me, that's crazily simplistic. **In reality, the type of assets you own should be matched to what *you* personally need to accomplish.** After all, a 55-year-old single mom who is saving for her kid's college tuition has different priorities than a 55-year-old entrepreneur who's just sold her business for millions and wants to build a philanthropic legacy. It makes no sense to treat them as if their needs are the same just because they're the same age!

Another common approach involves basing a person's asset allocation on his or her tolerance for risk. As the client, you fill out a questionnaire to establish whether you're an aggressive or conservative investor. You're then sold a prepackaged model investment portfolio that supposedly matches this risk profile. To me, this approach is equally misguided because it ignores your needs. What if you're risk averse but have no chance of retiring unless you invest heavily in stocks? Setting you up with a conservative portfolio loaded with bonds would just doom you to disappointment.

So how *should* you approach the challenge of asset allocation? As I see it, the real question that you and your financial advisor have to answer is this: **What asset classes will give you the highest probability of getting from where you are today to where you *need* to be?** In other words, the design of your portfolio must be based on *your specific needs*.

Your advisor should start by getting a clear picture of where you are today (your starting point), how much you're willing and able to save, how much money you'll need, and when you'll need it (your ending point). Once these needs have been clearly identified, your advisor should provide a *customized* solution to help you achieve them. Can you figure all of this out yourself, without hiring a professional? Sure. But the stakes are high, and you don't want to mess up. So it probably makes sense to get help, unless you're particularly knowledgeable about these matters.

In any case, let's say you need an average annual return of 7% over the next 15 years so you can retire. Your advisor might conclude that you ought to invest, say, 75% of your portfolio in stocks and 25% in bonds. It doesn't matter if you're 50 or 60 years old. Remember: your *needs* determine your asset allocation, not your *age*. Once your advisor has settled on the right allocation to meet those needs, you should discuss whether you can live with the volatility you're likely to experience. If you *can't*, then you can adjust your goal downward, and your advisor can create a more conservative allocation that allows you to achieve this scaled-back goal.

A sophisticated advisor will customize your portfolio to address whatever is unique about your financial situation. Let's say you work for an oil company and have a hefty portion of your net worth in your employer's stock. Your advisor would adjust your asset allocation accordingly to ensure that your other investments don't expose you too heavily to the energy sector.

Another priority is to create a customized game plan that minimizes your tax liabilities. Let's say you show an existing portfolio to a new advisor. Your asset allocation is clearly out of whack, so the advisor suggests a total overhaul. In a perfect world, he or she may be right. But what if your investments have done well, and selling them would saddle you with a big tax bill on all your capital gains? A sophisticated advisor would first assess the tax impact of selling these assets. As a result, you might end up taking a much slower approach—for example, using your additional monthly contributions to build more gradually toward your new allocation.

The point is, you want an advisor with the skills to tailor your portfolio to suit your specific needs. A one-size-fits-all approach to asset allocation can be disastrous. It would be like going to a doctor who tells you, "This drug I'm giving you is the best arthritis treatment in the world." Your reply: "That's great, Doc, but I don't have arthritis! I've got a cold."

CORE AND EXPLORE

Before we wrap up this chapter, I want to leave you with a few key guidelines to keep in mind when you're constructing (or reconstructing) your portfolio. These are principles we live by at Creative Planning, and I'm confident that they'll serve you well through sunny days and storms!

1. **Asset Allocation Drives Returns.** Let's start with the fundamental understanding that your asset allocation will be the biggest factor in determining your investment returns. **So, deciding on the right balance of stocks, bonds, and alternatives is the most important investment decision you'll ever make.** Whatever mix you choose, make sure you diversify globally across multiple asset classes. Imagine being a Japanese investor with all your money in domestic stocks: Japan's market is *still* down from the insane heights it reached in 1989. **The moral: never bet your future on one country or one asset class.**

2. **Use Index Funds for the Core of Your Portfolio.** At Creative Planning, we use an approach to asset allocation that we call "Core and Explore." The *core* component of our clients' portfolios is invested in US and international stocks. We use index funds because they give you broad diversification in a low-cost, tax-efficient way, and they beat almost all actively managed funds over the long run. For maximum diversification, we want exposure to stocks of all sizes: large-cap, midcap, small-cap, and microcap. By diversifying so broadly, you protect yourself against the risk that one part of the market (say, tech stocks or bank stocks) could get crushed. By indexing, you enjoy the long-term upward trajectory of the market without letting expenses and taxes corrode your returns. For other parts of your portfolio, there are more sophisticated options to consider, as we will discuss later.

3. **Always Have a Cushion.** You never want to be in a position where you're forced to sell your stock market investments at the worst moment. So it makes sense to maintain a financial cushion, if at all possible. We make sure our clients have an appropriate amount of income-producing investments such as bonds, REITs, MLPs, and dividend-paying stocks. We also diversify broadly *within* these asset classes: for example, we

invest in government bonds, muni bonds, and corporate bonds. If stocks crash, we can sell some of those income-producing investments (ideally bonds, since they are liquid) and use the proceeds to invest in the stock market at low prices. This puts us in a strong position where we can view the bear as a friend rather than a fearsome enemy.

4. **The Rule of Seven.** Ideally, we like our clients to have seven years of income set aside in income-producing investments such as bonds and MLPs. If stocks crash, we can tap these income-producing assets to meet our clients' short-term needs. But what if you can't afford to set aside years of income? Simply start with an achievable goal and keep raising the bar as you progress. For example, you might start with a goal of saving three or six months of income, and then work your way—over many years—toward the ultimate goal of setting aside seven years of income. If that sounds impossible, check out the wonderful story of Theodore Johnson, a UPS worker who never earned more than $14,000 a year. He saved 20% of every paycheck, plus every bonus, and invested in his company's stock. By age 90, he'd accumulated $70 million! **The lesson: never underestimate the awesome power of disciplined saving combined with long-term compounding.**

5. **Explore.** The *core* of our clients' portfolios is invested in index funds that simply match the market's return. But at the margins, it can make sense to *explore* additional strategies that offer a reasonable chance of outperformance. For example, a wealthy investor might add a high-risk, high-return investment in a private equity fund. You might also decide that a particular investor like Warren Buffett has a specific advantage, which could justify putting a modest portion of your portfolio in shares of his company, Berkshire Hathaway.

6. **Rebalance.** I'm a big believer in "rebalancing," which entails bringing your portfolio back to your original asset allocation on a regular basis— say, once a year. At Creative Planning, we take opportunities to buy as they happen, rather than waiting for the end of the year or quarter. Here is how it works: imagine you start with 60% in stocks and 40% in bonds; then the stock market plunges, so you find yourself with 45% in stocks and 55% in bonds. You'd rebalance by selling bonds and buying stocks. **As Princeton professor Burton Malkiel told Tony,**

unsuccessful investors tend to "buy the thing that's gone up and sell the thing that's gone down." One benefit of rebalancing, says Malkiel, is that it "makes you do the opposite," forcing you to buy assets when they're out of favor and undervalued. You'll profit richly when they recover.

A FINAL WORD

If you follow the advice in this chapter, you'll be able to ride out any storm. Sure, there'll be turbulent times when the news is full of frightening headlines. But you'll have the comfort of knowing that your portfolio is properly diversified, so it can withstand any market mayhem.

In chapter 2, you learned that there's no need to fear market corrections, and I hope you see now that there's no need to fear bear markets, either. In fact, they provide the best opportunity to buy the bargains of a lifetime, so you can leapfrog to a whole new level of wealth. The bear is your gift—one that comes, on average, once every three years! These aren't just times to survive. These are times to *thrive*.

But as you and I both know, there's a big difference between theory and practice. Just think of my former client who cashed out of the stock market and gambled everything on gold during the last bear market. Fear led him to jettison a carefully constructed plan that would have ensured him a future of total financial freedom. So how can you make sure that your own emotions won't get out of hand and knock you off course?

The next chapter will focus on how to master the psychology of wealth so you won't make the common—and entirely avoidable—financial mistakes we see again and again. As you'll discover, there's only one real barrier to financial success: you! Once you know how to silence the enemy within, nothing can stop you.

THE PSYCHOLOGY OF WEALTH

CHAPTER 8

SILENCING THE ENEMY WITHIN

*The Six Money Mistakes Investors Make
and How You Can Avoid Them*

The investor's chief problem—and even his
worst enemy—is likely to be himself.
—BENJAMIN GRAHAM, author of *The Intelligent Investor*
and mentor to Warren Buffett

Congratulations! You've made it through the rule book and the playbook and now possess the knowledge you need to become truly unshakeable.

You've learned what you need to watch out for, you've learned the facts that can free you from the fear of the inevitable corrections and crashes, and you're fully armed with the winning strategies of the best investors on the planet. You've also acquired invaluable knowledge about fees, and how to find a truly qualified and effective financial advisor. All of this gives you an amazing edge, vastly enhancing your ability to remain clear-headed even in the face of uncertainty. You have a proven pathway to financial freedom!

But I have to ask . . . What could mess this up?

I'll give you a clue: it's nothing external. *It's you!* **That's right. The single biggest threat to your financial well-being is your own brain.** I'm not trying to insult you here! It's just that the human brain is perfectly designed to make dumb decisions when it comes to investing. You can do everything right—invest in low-cost index funds, minimize fees and taxes, and diversify intelligently. But if you fail to master your own psychology, you may ultimately become the victim of a costly form of financial self-sabotage.

In fact, this is part of a much broader pattern. In every area of life—whether it's dating, marriage, parenting, the workplace, our health, our fitness, our finances, or anything else—we have a tendency to be our own worst enemy.

The problem is that our brains are wired to avoid pain and seek pleasure. Instinctively, we yearn for whatever feels likely to be immediately rewarding. Needless to say, this isn't always the best recipe for smart decision making.

In fact, our brains are particularly prone to bad decisions when we're dealing with money.

As we'll discuss, there's an array of mental biases—or blind spots—that make it surprisingly difficult to invest rationally. It's not our fault. It's part of being human. In fact, it's built into the system inside your head, like a piece of faulty code in a computer program.

This chapter is designed to give you the key insights and tools you can use to free yourself from the natural psychological tendencies that derail so many people on the journey toward financial freedom.

Let me give you an example of a common psychological obstacle that we're all likely to encounter. **Neuroscientists have found that the parts of the brain that process financial losses are the same parts that respond to mortal threats.** Think about what that means for a moment. Imagine you're a hunter-gatherer searching for dinner in the forest when you're suddenly confronted by a saber-toothed tiger with a serious attitude problem. Your brain goes into high alert, sending you urgent messages to fight, freeze, or run for your life. You might grab the nearest rock or spear so you can battle the beast, or you might flee and hide out in the safety of a dark cave.

Now imagine that it's 2008, and you're an investor with a big chunk of your life savings in the stock market. The global financial crisis slams the market, your investments take a tumble, and your brain begins to process the reality that you're losing heaps of money. As far as your brain is concerned, this is the financial equivalent of that saber-toothed tiger roaring in your face, ready to make *you* his dinner.

So what happens? Red alert! The ancient survival mechanism inside your brain starts sending you messages that you're in mortal danger. Rationally, you may know that the smartest move in a market crash is to buy more stocks while they're on sale. But your brain is telling you to sell everything, grab your cash, and hide under your bed (more convenient than a cave) until the threat subsides. It's no wonder that most investors do the wrong thing! It's an unfortunate side effect of the human survival mechanism. We have a tendency to freak out because our brains believe our financial downfall is *certain death*.

And what counts is not reality, but rather our beliefs about it.

Our beliefs are what deliver direct commands to our nervous system. Beliefs are nothing but feelings of absolute certainty governing our behavior. Handled effectively, beliefs can be the most powerful force for creating good, but our beliefs can also limit our choices and hamstring our actions severely. So what's the solution? How can we bypass the survival instincts that have been hardwired into our brains and belief systems for millions of years, so we can learn to stand firm in the face of a plunging market (or a hungry tiger)?

It may seem overly simplistic, but all that's really required is a set of system solutions—a simple system of checks and balances—to neutralize or minimize the harmful effects of our faulty Flintstone wiring. There has to be a kind of internal control checklist since knowing is not enough. You need the systemic ability to *execute every time.*

Just think of the airline industry, where the consequences of human error can be devastating. For airlines, it's imperative that they follow the correct procedures *every* time. So they minimize risks by implementing a series of system solutions and a series of checklists along the way. Consider the copilot, who provides an array of potentially life-saving checks and balances, just in case the pilot slips up. The copilot isn't just there to merely steer the plane if the captain is in the washroom, but also serves as a second opinion for every decision point that may arise. Plus, it doesn't matter how many thousands of hours they've flown—both the pilot and copilot constantly monitor detailed checklists to keep everybody safely on course, so they'll arrive at their intended destination.

When it comes to investing, human error may not be a matter of life and death, but financial mistakes can still be catastrophic. Just ask those who lost their homes during the financial crisis, or couldn't pay for their kids to stay in college, or can't afford to retire. **This is why investors also need simple systems, rules, and procedures to protect us from ourselves.**

KNOW WHAT TO DO, DO WHAT YOU KNOW

The best investors are acutely aware of this need for simple systems because they recognize that, despite their abundant talents, they can easily mess up in ways that could cause them a world of pain! **They understand that it's**

not enough to *know what to do.* **You also need to** *do what you know.* That's where systems come in.

Over my 20 plus years as a coach to Paul Tudor Jones, a key focus has been to constantly update and improve the systems he uses to evaluate and make investment decisions. In fact, when I first met Paul, he had just made one of the greatest investment trades in history, taking full advantage of the market on Black Monday in 1987—an infamous occasion when the market fell 22% in a single day. Paul produced an almost unimaginable return of 200% that year for his investors. But after this stunning success, he became overconfident—a common bias that you'll learn more about in this chapter. The result? He became less rigorous in his adherence to the vital systems he'd accumulated over the years to become his most effective self.

In order to correct this bias, I set out to discover how his behavior as an investor had changed. I met with Paul's peers (including some of the greatest investors in history, such as Stanley Druckenmiller), interviewed his coworkers, and watched videos of him trading during his most successful times. Based on this in-depth understanding, I worked with Paul to create a checklist: a simple set of criteria that he could use as his checks and balances before making any trade.

For example, one of the criteria we established was that before he could make any investment (or trade), Paul had to first establish in his own heart and soul that it was a *hard trade*—meaning it wasn't a trade that everyone would make.

Second, he disciplined himself to make sure that there was asymmetrical risk/reward. In order to determine this, he would ask himself: *"Is it a three-to-one? Is it a five-to-one? Can I get disproportionate rewards for the least amount of risk? What's the potential upside and what's the risk on the downside?"* Third, he would sit down and ask himself, *"Where are the breaking points for other investors? When will the price get so low or high that they will get out?"* He would then use this insight to establish his own entry point: his target price for executing his investment. And finally, he would also establish his exit if his projections turned out to be wrong.

What's the pattern here? **The common link in Paul's criteria is a simple set of** *questions* **that he uses to examine his beliefs and look at the situation more objectively.**

And while all of these questions have provided a great checklist for Paul, what made it work was *discipline*. After all, a system is effective only if you use it! In order to be sure that he did, I asked Paul to write a letter to the members of his entire trading team stating clearly that they were not to make any investment until they checked with him first and asked the questions we outlined above: *"Is this truly the hard trade? Does it really have asymmetric risk/reward? Is it a five-to-one or a three-to-one? What's the entry point? Where are your stops?"*

To take it one step further, they were also instructed not to process any orders after the opening bell. In other words, they weren't allowed to trade in the middle of the day. Why not? Because Paul realized that too often a trade in that stage of the game meant that he was reacting to the market, buying at the high price for the day and selling at the low, giving away his power and gifting someone else a better deal.

As you can see, great investors such as Paul understand a fundamental truth: psychology either makes you or breaks you, so it's imperative to have a robust system that enables you to stay on target. Together in this chapter, were going to create a simple checklist with six items to watch out for and effectively counter to insure your long-term financial success.

80% PSYCHOLOGY,
20% MECHANICS

For four decades, I've studied the most successful people in many different fields, including investing, business, education, sports, medicine, and entertainment. **And what I've found again and again is that 80% of success is psychology and 20% is mechanics.**

Investor psychology is an incredibly rich and complex subject. In fact, there's an entire academic field called "behavioral finance," which explores the cognitive biases and emotions that cause investors to act irrationally. These biases often lead people to make some of the costliest investing mistakes, such as trying to time the market, investing without knowledge of the real impact of fees, and failing to diversify.

Our goal here is to keep things short and sweet! In this brief

chapter, we're going to explain what you *really* need to know about one of the biggest psychological pitfalls and how to avoid getting snagged by common investment mistakes your brain can cause you to make.

As Ray Dalio told me, "If you know your limitations, you can adapt and succeed. If you don't know them, you're going to get hurt." By creating systematic solutions, you can free yourself from the tyranny of your conditioning and operate the control room like one of the best investors on the planet.

Mistake 1: Seeking Confirmation of Your Beliefs
Why the Best Investors Welcome Opinions That Contradict Their Own

During the 2016 presidential election battle between Donald Trump and Hillary Clinton, you probably found yourself in heated political "debates" with friends. But did you ever have the feeling that it wasn't a debate at all—that everyone had made up his or her mind already? People who loved Trump and loathed Hillary, or vice versa, felt so strongly that it often seemed like nothing could alter their opinions!

This was magnified by the way we consume media today. Many people watch TV channels that typically favor one point of view, such as MSNBC or Fox News; and our news is filtered more than ever by Facebook and other organizations. The result? It often feels like we're in an echo chamber, listening primarily to people who share our views.

The 2016 election provided a perfect example of "confirmation bias," which is the human tendency to seek out and value information that confirms our own preconceptions and beliefs. This tendency also leads us to avoid, undervalue, or disregard any information that conflicts with our beliefs.

For investors, confirmation bias is a dangerous predisposition.

Let's say you love a particular stock or fund that's performed exceptionally well in your portfolio over the last year. Your brain is wired to seek out and believe information that validates you owning it. After all, our minds love proof—especially proof of how smart and right we've been!

Investors often visit newsletters and message boards that reinforce their beliefs about the stocks they own. Or they pump their accelerator by reading positive articles about the hot sector where they've been earning fabulous returns. But what if the situation changes and that high-flying stock or sector starts crashing back to earth? How well equipped are we to change our perspective and recognize that we've made a mistake?

Do you have the flexibility to change your approach, or is your mind locked into its beliefs?

Peter Mallouk saw this phenomenon up close with a new client who had previously made a fortune on a biotech stock that had skyrocketed over a decade. The client had almost $10 million in this one stock. Peter and his team at Creative Planning set up an efficient plan for the client to diversify, dramatically reducing her exposure to this stock. The client agreed initially but then changed her mind, claiming she "knew" her beloved stock and understood why it would continue to soar. She told Peter, "I don't care what you're saying. This stock is what got me here!"

Over the next four months, Peter's team kept trying to convince her to begin the diversification process. But the client wouldn't listen. During that time, the stock dropped by half, costing her $5 million. She was so upset that she dug in her heels even more and insisted on waiting for the stock to recover. It never did. If she had listened to this well-considered advice that contradicted her own beliefs, she would now likely be on track toward a life of total financial freedom.

In fact, this is also an example of another emotional bias called the "endowment effect," in which investors place greater value on something they already own, regardless of its objective value! This makes it much harder to part ways and buy something superior. The truth is, it's never wise to fall in love with an investment. As the saying goes, love is blind! Don't get swept off your financial feet.

The Solution: Ask Better Questions and Find Qualified People Who Disagree with You

The best investors know they're vulnerable to confirmation bias and, accordingly, do everything they can to counter this tendency. **The key is to actively seek out qualified opinions that differ from your own. Of course, you don't want just anyone with a different opinion, but rather**

someone who has the skill, track record, and intelligence to give another educated perspective. All opinions are not created equal.

Nobody understands this better than Warren Buffett. He consults regularly with his 93-year-old partner, Charlie Munger, a brilliant thinker who is also famously outspoken. In his 2014 annual report, Buffett recalled that Munger had single-handedly convinced him to change his investment strategy, persuading him that there was a smarter approach: "Forget what you know about buying fair businesses at wonderful prices; instead, buy wonderful businesses at fair prices."

In other words, Warren Buffett—the greatest investor in history—has openly attributed his success to his willingness to follow the advice of his partner, whose "logic was irrefutable." That's how powerful it can be to resist our tendency to seek opinions that merely confirm our own!

Ray Dalio, too, is obsessed with the idea of searching for divergent viewpoints. **"It's so difficult to be right in the markets," he told me. "So what I've found very effective is to find people who disagree with me and then find out what their reasoning is. . . . The power of thoughtful disagreement is a great thing." As Ray explains, the key question is: "What don't I know?"**

You can benefit greatly as an investor by finding people you respect (ideally, this includes a financial advisor with an extraordinary long-term record) and asking them questions designed to uncover what you don't know. Whenever I'm contemplating a major investment, I speak with friends who think differently, including my wise pal and genius entrepreneur, Peter Guber. I explain what I believe, and then I ask: *"Where could I be wrong? What am I not seeing? What's the downside? What am I failing to anticipate? And who else should I speak with to deepen my knowledge?"* Questions like these help to protect me from the danger of confirmation bias.

Mistake 2: Mistaking Recent Events for Ongoing Trends
Why Most Investors Buy the Wrong Thing at Exactly the Wrong Moment

One of the most common—and dangerous—investing mistakes is the belief that the current trend will continue. And when investors' expectations aren't met, they often overreact, leading to a dramatic reversal of the trend that previously seemed inevitable and unstoppable.

A perfect example of this phenomenon occurred election night in 2016. Hillary Clinton, by far the front-runner, was expected to win by a landslide—or at least by a "significant margin" according to nearly every poll. At noon on election day, bookies around the country gave her a 61% chance of victory. But by eight o'clock, the situation flip-flopped completely, giving Trump a 90% chance of winning. As the election results became clear, investors panicked because their expectations about the future were suddenly turned upside down. The market responded violently, with Dow futures dropping more than 900 points.

Ironically, the next day, the market snapped back in the opposite direction, with the Dow jumping 316 points as investors began to adjust to their new version of reality. We witnessed a Trump rally that continued for weeks. As I write this in December 2016, the S&P 500 just hit an all-time high for the third day in a row, the Dow Jones Industrial Average has scored its eleventh all-time high in a month, and the market has surged 6% in 7 weeks since the election!

How do you think investors feel right now? Pretty cheerful, that's how! When you read that the market is "roaring ahead," it's hard not to feel a little rush of delight! Maybe you peek at your investment portfolio and notice that it's the highest it's ever been. Life is sweet!

Granted, I have no idea where the market is headed from here, and as the greatest investors in the world will tell you, neither does anyone else! But I *do* know that people get carried away at times like this. In the stacking of emotions and beliefs they start to convince themselves that the good times will keep on rolling! Likewise, when the market is plunging, they start to believe that it will never recover. As Warren Buffett says: "Investors project out into the future what they have most recently been seeing. That is their unshakeable habit."

What's the explanation for this? **There's actually a technical term for this psychological habit. It's called "recency bias." This is just a posh way of saying that recent experiences carry more weight in our minds when we're evaluating the odds of something happening in the future.**

In the midst of a bull market, the neurons in your brain help you to remember that your recent experiences were positive, and this creates an expectation that the positive trend is likely to continue!

Why is this so problematic? Because, as you know, the financial seasons can suddenly change, with bull markets giving way to bear markets and vice versa. You don't want to be that guy who, after a long, sun-drenched summer, concludes that it'll never rain again.

> Great things are not accomplished by those who
> yield to trends and fads and popular opinion.
> —JACK KEROUAC

I recently interviewed Harry Markowitz, a famous economist who won the Nobel Prize for developing "modern portfolio theory": the basis for much of what we know today about how to use asset allocation to reduce risk. Harry is a financial genius, and, at the age of 89, he's seen everything under the sun, so I was eager to speak with him about the most common investing mistakes we need to avoid.

Here's what he told me: "The biggest mistake that the small investor makes is to buy when the market is going up on the assumption that the market will go up further—and sell when the market is going down on the assumption that it's going to go down further."

In fact, this is part of a much broader pattern of believing that current investment trends are bound to continue. Investors repeatedly fall into the trap of buying what's hot—whether it's a high-flying stock like Tesla Motors or the latest five-star mutual fund—and abandoning what's not. As Harry puts it: "Whatever is going up, *that's* what they buy!" People assume that these shooting stars will continue to burn brightly. But as we warned in chapter 3, *today's winners tend to be tomorrow's losers*. As you may recall, one study looked at 248 stock funds that received Morningstar's five-star rating. Ten years later, only *four* of them kept that rank!

Even so, brokers routinely promote funds that outperformed in the previous year, only to see these recommendations *underperform* the following year. Investors tend to arrive just as the party is winding down. They miss out on all of the gains and participate fully in all of the losses. David

Swensen summed this up neatly, telling me, **"Individuals tend to buy funds that have good performance. And they chase returns. And then, when funds perform poorly, they sell. And so they end up buying high and selling low. And that's a bad way to make money."**

The Solution: Don't Sell Out. Rebalance.

What the best investors in the world do is create a list of simple rules to guide them so that when things get emotional, they stay the course and remain on-target long term. You might want to start making a list of your own—*an investment success checklist for the flight deck*—that spells out where you're trying to go as an investor, what you have to watch out for, and how you plan to navigate the journey securely. Share your flight plan with someone you trust—ideally, a sophisticated financial advisor. He or she can help you stick with the program by making sure you don't violate your own rules with impulsive survival-brain decisions. **Think of this as the financial equivalent of having a copilot to clarify and verify that you're not heading into the side of a mountain!**

An important component of these investment rules is deciding in advance how you're going to diversify by allocating a specific percentage of your portfolio to stocks, bonds, and alternative investments. What will your ratio be?[17] If you don't lock it down, circumstances will change and your mood will change with them. You're likely to react to the moment, instead of sticking consistently with an asset allocation that's ideal for you over time. If you recall, one of the solutions to this emotional stumbling block is to regularly rebalance your portfolio once a year.

What does that mean? Harry Markowitz gave me a clear example of an investor who starts with 60% of her portfolio in stocks and 40% in bonds. If the stock market soars, she might find herself with 70% in stocks and 30% in bonds. So she would automatically sell stocks and buy bonds, thereby restoring her portfolio to her original asset allocation ratio. The beauty of

---

17 If you'd like more guidance in this area, Chapter 4.1 of *Money: Master the Game* gives you simple step-by-step guidance in how to set your asset allocation percentages.

rebalancing, says Harry, is that it effectively forces you to "buy low and sell high."

Mistake 3: Overconfidence
Get Real: Overestimating Our Abilities and
Our Knowledge Is a Recipe for Disaster!

Forgive me for getting personal here, but let me ask you three questions. Are you an above-average driver? Are you an above-average lover? And are you better-looking than the average person? Don't worry! You can keep your answers to yourself!

My reason for asking you these impertinent questions is to raise a fundamental point that could be vitally important to your financial future: humans have a perilous tendency to believe that they're better (or smarter) than they really are. Again, there's a technical term for this psychological bias: it's called "overconfidence." To put it simply, we consistently overestimate our abilities, our knowledge, and our future prospects.

Countless studies have described some of the wonderfully absurd effects of overconfidence. For example, one study found that 93% of student drivers believe they are above average. In another study, 94% of college professors considered themselves above average in the classroom. There was even a finding that 79% of students believed their character was better than most, despite the fact that 60% admitted they had cheated on an exam in the previous year. We each envision ourselves as a member of the "*I'd never do that*" moral minority.

All this reminds me of Lake Wobegon, the fictitious Minnesota town invented by the writer Garrison Keillor, "where all the women are strong, all the men are good-looking, and all the children are above average."

So how do individual investors become overconfident? In many cases, a "professional" convinces them that there is a hot new investment that's going to crush everything out there, and they allow that person's passion to become their unwarranted confidence. In other words, one person's salesmanship fuels another person's misguided certainty.

Some individuals are extremely successful in running a business or living their lives, so they just assume that they'll be equally as effective as an investor. But investing, as you know now, is more complex and challenging than it might initially seem to these high achievers.

Are certain people more prone to overconfidence? Finance professors Brad Barber and Terrance Odean examined the stock investments of more than 35 thousand households over five years. **They found that men are especially prone to overconfidence when it comes to investing! In fact,** *men traded 45% more than women,* **reducing their net returns by 2.65% a year!** When you add to this the additional costs of high transaction fees and taxes, you can see that excessive trading is truly a disaster.

But there's another form of overconfidence that can prove even more costly; the perilous belief that you (or any TV pundit, market strategist, or blog writer) can predict what the future holds for the stock market, bonds, gold, oil, or any other asset class. "If you can't predict the future, the most important thing is to admit it," Howard Marks told me. "If it's true that you can't make forecasts and yet you try anyway, then that's really suicide."

The Solution: Get Real, Get Honest

One of the best antidotes to overconfidence is to stand in front of a mirror and ask yourself this: "Do I really have an edge that will allow me to be a market-beating investor?" Unless you have some secret sauce—for example, the superior information and analytical skills that distinguish great investors such as Howard Marks, Warren Buffett, and Ray Dalio—there's no rational reason on earth to believe you can outperform the market indexes over the long run.

So what should you do? Easy! Do what Howard, Warren, Jack Bogle, David Swensen, and other of the world's greatest investors tell the average investor to do: invest in a portfolio of low-cost index funds, and then hold them through thick and thin. This will give you the market's return, without the triple burden that active investors must carry: exorbitant management fees, high transaction costs, and hefty tax bills. "If you can't add value, if you can't create an asymmetry, then the best thing you can do is minimize your costs," says Howard. In other words, "Just invest in an index."

Index funds also give you broad diversification, which is another powerful protection against overconfidence. After all, diversification is an admission that you don't know which particular asset class, which stock or bond, or which country will do best. So you own a bit of everything!

Here's the great paradox: *by admitting to yourself that you have no special advantage, you give yourself an enormous advantage!* **How come? Because you'll do so much better than all those overconfident investors who delude themselves into believing they can outperform.** When it comes to investing, self-deception may be the biggest expense of all!

Mistake 4: Greed, Gambling, and the Quest for Home Runs
It's Tempting to Swing for the Fences, but
Victory Goes to the Steady Survivors

When I was 19, I rented a house in an upscale community by the Pacific Ocean in Marina del Rey, California. One day I was dropping off some clothes at a local dry cleaner when a convertible Rolls-Royce Corniche pulled up, and a gorgeous woman stepped out. I couldn't help but pay attention! We started chatting while she picked up her clothes, and I asked what she and her family did for a living. She told me that her husband was in penny stocks and had done really well. "I can see that," I said. "Do you have any tips?"

She replied, "Actually, right now, there's an extraordinary one." She gave me the name of a hot stock—and let me tell you, it felt like a gift from on high! A sure thing, right from the horse's mouth! So I took $3,000, which was the equivalent of $3 million for me back then, and I bet it all on that one stock. And guess what happened? It went to zero! Boy, did I feel like an idiot.

As I learned from that painful experience, greed and impatience are dangerous traits when it comes to investing. We all have a tendency to want the biggest and best results as fast as possible, rather than focusing on small, incremental changes that compound over time. **The best way to win the game of investing is to achieve *sustainable* long-term returns. But it's enormously tempting to swing for home runs, especially when you think other people are getting rich faster than you!**

The trouble is, you're more liable to strike out when you swing for the fences. And that can be devastating. As we discussed in chapter 6, all of the best investors are obsessed with the idea of not losing. Remember our math lesson? When you lose 50% on an investment, you need a 100% return just to get back to where you started—and that could easily take you a decade.

Unfortunately, the desire to gamble is built into us. The gaming industry knows this well and ingeniously exploits our physiology and psychology: when we're winning, our bodies release chemicals called endorphins, so we feel euphoric and don't want to stop; when we're losing, we don't want to stop either, since we crave those endorphins and also want to avoid the emotional pain of losses. Casinos know how to manipulate us by pumping in extra oxygen to keep us alert and by plying us with free drinks to reduce our inhibitions! After all, the more we play, the more they'll win.

Wall Street isn't all that different! Brokerage houses love it when customers trade a lot, generating a blizzard of fees. They try to lure you in and hook you with advertisements that offer free or low-cost trades, along with market "insights" that will supposedly help you pick the winners. Yeah, right! Do you think it's a coincidence that your online trading platform looks and sounds like a casino, with green and red colors, scrolling tickers, flashing images, and dinging sounds? It's all designed to unleash your inner speculator!

The financial media reinforces the sense that the markets are just one giant casino—an intoxicating get-rich-quick scheme for speculators! It's easy to get sucked in, which is why so many people lose their shirts by betting on the hottest stocks, trading options, and moving in and out of the market. All this activity is motivated by the gambler's desire to hit the jackpot!

What you need to understand is that there's a world of difference between short-term speculation and long-term investing. Speculators are doomed to fail, while disciplined investors who stay in the market through thick and thin set themselves up for victory, thanks to the power of compounding over time. Wall Street wins by getting you to be more active, but *you* win by patiently staying in the game for decades. **Remember, as Warren Buffett says, "The stock market is a device for transferring money from the impatient to the patient."**

The Solution: It's a Marathon, Not a Sprint

So here's the big question: *In practical terms, how can you silence your inner speculator and force yourself to be a patient, long-term investor?*

One person who's obsessed with this question is Guy Spier, a renowned value investor. Guy began coming to my events two decades ago, and he credits me with inspiring him to model the best investors. He applied this idea by modeling Warren Buffett's long-term approach to investing. In 2008 Guy and another hedge fund manager even paid $650,100 to charity to have lunch with Buffett!

As Guy sees it, one of the biggest barriers to success for most investors is that they get distracted by all the short-term noise on Wall Street. This makes it much harder for them to hold their investments for the long run and harness the awesome power of compounding. For example, they frequently check the performance of their investments, and they listen to TV pundits and market "experts" making useless predictions. "When you check your stock prices or fund prices on your computer every day, you're feeding candy to your brain," says Guy. "You get an endorphin hit. You have to realize it's addictive behavior and just stop doing it. Move away from the candy!"

Guy suggests checking your portfolio only *once a year*. He recommends avoiding financial TV entirely. And he suggests that you disregard all research produced by Wall Street firms, recognizing that their motive is to push products, not to share wisdom! "The vast majority of what purports to be analysis and information about the stock market is actually just designed to generate activity, to get us to pull the trigger because somebody out there will make money out of the fact that we're being active," he explains. "If it's activity-generating information, we should shut it off."

Instead, Guy recommends creating "a more wholesome information diet" by studying the wisdom of ultrapatient investors such as Warren Buffett and Jack Bogle. The result? "You're feeding your mind thoughts that will make it much easier for you to think and act long term."

Mistake 5: Staying Home
It's a Big World out There—So How Come Most Investors Stay So Close to Home?

Humans have a natural tendency to stay within their comfort zone. If you live in the United States, you're more likely to crave a cheeseburger with fries than a feast consisting of foie gras, poutine, or escargot. Likewise, you probably have a favorite grocery store, gas station, or coffee shop that you visit regularly, instead of venturing further afield.

When it comes to investing, people also tend to stick with whatever they know best, preferring to trust what's most familiar. This is known as "home bias." It's a psychological bias that leads people to invest disproportionately in their own country's markets—and sometimes to invest too heavily in their employer's stock and their own industry.

For our cave-dwelling ancestors, home bias was a savvy survival strategy. If you ventured too far outside the 'hood, who knew what dangers might be lying in wait? But in our own era, investing globally actually reduces your overall risk. That's because different markets are imperfectly correlated, which means they don't move in lockstep.

You don't want to be overexposed to *any* country—even if it's where you live—because you never know when it will hit a rough patch. In the late 1980s, Japanese investors had 98% of their portfolios in domestic stocks. This paid off handsomely for most of the eighties, when Japan seemed to be on top of the world. Then in 1989 the Japanese market collapsed, and it's never fully recovered. So much for "Home, sweet home!"

A report by Morningstar showed that the average American investor in mutual funds had almost three-quarters (73%) of his or her total equity allocation invested in the US stock market at the end of 2013. Yet US stocks accounted for only half (49%) of the global equity market. In other words, Americans significantly overweighted the US market, leaving them relatively underexposed to foreign markets such as the United Kingdom, Germany, China, and India.

In fact, it's not just American investors who view the rest of the world with suspicion! Richard Thaler and Cass Sunstein, who are leading experts on behavioral finance, have written that Swedish investors have an average of 48% of their money in Swedish stocks—despite the fact that Sweden accounts for around 1% of the global economy: "A rational investor in the United States or Japan would invest about 1% of his assets in Swedish stocks. Can it make sense for Swedish investors to invest 48 times more? No."

The Solution: Expand Your Horizons

This is *really* simple. As we've said in previous chapters, you need to diversify broadly, not only in different asset classes but also in different countries. It makes sense to discuss your global asset allocation with a financial advisor. Once you've decided on the appropriate percentages to keep at home and abroad, you should write down these figures in your investment success checklist. It's also important to lay out, in writing, the reasons why you own what you own. That way, you can remind yourself of these reasons whenever a part of your portfolio is underperforming.

The best advisors help you to keep a long-term perspective so you can avoid falling into the common trap of favoring whatever market is in vogue. Harry Markowitz, who has a deep sense of history, told me, "We've recently had a long stretch where the US market has been doing better than the European market . . . and emerging markets have had a dry spell. But these things come and go."

By diversifying internationally, you're not only reducing your overall risk but also increasing your returns. Remember when we talked about the "lost decade" of 2000 through 2009, when the S&P 500 produced an annualized return of only 1.4% a year, including dividends? During that time, international stocks averaged 3.9% a year, while emerging-market stocks returned 16.2% a year. So, for investors who diversified globally, those lost years were just a minor bump in the road.

Mistake 6: Negativity and Loss Aversion
Your Brain Wants You to Be Fearful in Times
of Turmoil—Don't Listen to It!

Human beings have a natural tendency to recall negative experiences more vividly than they do positive ones. This is known as "negativity bias." Back when we were cavemen, this mental bias was really handy. It helped us to remember that fire hurts, that certain berries could poison us, and that it was dumb to pick a fight with a hunter twice your size. Recalling negative experiences can also be pretty helpful in modern times: maybe you forgot that it was your wedding anniversary, spent the next day in the doghouse, and thereby learned never to make that mistake again!

But how does negativity bias affect the way we invest? Thanks for asking! As you know, market corrections and bear markets are regular occurrences. **Remember: on average, corrections have occurred about once a year since 1900, and bear markets have occurred about once every three to five years.** If you lived through the bear market of 2008–09, you know firsthand how emotionally painful these experiences can be. If, like many investors, you owned funds or stocks that plunged by a third or a half (or more), you're not likely to forget those negative experiences anytime soon!

Now, you and I both know that the best investors *relish* corrections and bear markets because that's when everything goes on sale. By now, I'm sure you remember, Warren Buffett wants to be "greedy when others are fearful," and Sir John Templeton made his fortune—do you remember? That's right. At "the point of maximum pessimism." At this point, I'm guessing that your rational mind *knows* that market crashes are a wonderful opportunity to build long-term wealth, not something to fear! But negativity bias makes it hard for the average investor to *act* on this knowledge.

Why? Because in the midst of market turmoil, our brains are wired to bombard us with memories of those negative experiences. In fact, there's a part of the brain—the amygdala—that acts as a biological alarm system, flooding the body with fear signals when we're losing money! Even a minor market correction is liable to trigger our negative memories, causing many investors to overreact because they're afraid that the correction could turn into a crash. During a bear market, this fear reflex goes into overdrive, making investors anxious that the market will never recover!

To make matters worse, the psychologists Daniel Kahneman and Amos Tversky also demonstrated that financial losses cause people twice as much pain as the pleasure they receive from financial gains. The term used to describe this mental phenomenon is "loss aversion."

The trouble is, losing money causes investors so much pain that they tend to act irrationally just to avoid this possibility! For example, when the market is plunging, many people sell their battered investments and go to cash at exactly the wrong moment—instead of snapping up bargains at once-in-a-lifetime prices.

One reason why the best investors are so successful is that they override this natural tendency to be fearful during periods of market turmoil. Take Howard Marks. In the last 15 weeks of 2008, when financial markets were imploding, he told me that his team at Oaktree Capital Management invested about *$500 million a week* in distressed debt. **That's right! They invested half a billion dollars a week for 15 straight weeks during a time when many thought the end times had arrived! "It was obvious that everybody was suicidal," Howard told me. "In general, that's a good time to buy."**

By focusing calmly on this bargain-hunting opportunity, Howard and his teammates made billions of dollars in profits when winter ended and spring began. This would never have been possible if they had succumbed to fear!

The Solution: Preparation Is Key

By failing to *prepare*, you are *preparing* to fail.
—BENJAMIN FRANKLIN

First of all, it's important to be self-aware. Once we *know* that we're vulnerable to negativity bias and loss aversion, we can counter these psychological tendencies. After all, you can't change something if you're not aware of it! But what specific measures can you take so that fear won't knock you off course even in the most tumultuous times?

As we discussed in chapter 7, Peter Mallouk had tremendous success in helping his clients navigate the global financial crisis. One reason: He educated them in advance about the risks of a bear market, so it wasn't as surprising or scary when it actually occurred. For example, he explained how each asset class had performed in previous bear markets, so they were prepared mentally for what could happen.

They also knew in advance that Peter planned to use this turmoil to their advantage, selling conservative investments such as bonds and deploying the proceeds to buy more stocks at bargain prices. "We provided certainty about the process," says Peter, "so they knew exactly what to expect. This dramatically reduced their uncertainty." **In other words, the single best way to handle market turmoil—and the fears it can trigger—is to be prepared for it.**

As we've discussed at length, one critical way to prepare is to have the right asset allocation. It also helps to write down your reasons for investing in each of the assets in your portfolio, since inevitably there will be times a particular asset class or investment performs poorly, sometimes for several years. Many investors lose faith because they're so focused on the short term. But when the going gets tough, you'll be able to look over these notes and remind yourself why you own each asset and how it serves your long-term goals.

This simple process can take a lot of the heat and emotion out of investing. As long as your needs haven't changed and your assets are still aligned with your goals, you can sit tight and give your investments the time they need to prove their value.

It also helps immeasurably to have a financial advisor who can talk you through your fears and concerns during the most difficult times, reminding you that the strategy you agreed upon in writing when you were calm and unemotional is still valid.

It's a bit like flying a plane through a really rough storm. Most pilots would be just fine if they were flying solo. But it's a whole lot easier when you know that you've got an experienced copilot in the seat beside you! Remember: even Warren Buffett has a partner.

MASTERING YOUR MIND

Now that you're aware of these destructive psychological patterns, you're much better positioned to guard against them. Given that we're human beings, we're bound to trip up from time to time. After all, the biases we've discussed in this chapter are part of our ancient survival software, so we can't expect to eliminate them totally. But as Guy Spier says, "This isn't about getting a perfect score. Even small improvements in our behavior can deliver enormous rewards."

Why? Because investing is a game of inches. If your returns improve by, say, 2 or 3 percentage points a year, the cumulative impact over decades is astounding, thanks to the power of compounding. The systematic solutions we've discussed in this chapter will go a very long way, helping you to avoid—or minimize—the most expensive mistakes that the majority of investors make.

For example, these simple rules and procedures will make it easier for you to invest for the long term; to trade less; to lower your investment fees and transaction costs; to be more open to views that differ from your own; to reduce risk by diversifying globally; and to control the fears that could otherwise derail you during bear markets. Will you be perfect? No. But will you do better? You bet! And the difference this makes over a lifetime can amount to many millions of dollars!

Now you understand both the mechanics and the psychology of investing. You know what it takes to master your mind so that you can invest successfully over the long term. The knowledge you've acquired is priceless, and it can enable you and your family to achieve total financial freedom. So let's turn to our final chapter and learn how to create *real and lasting wealth*!

CHAPTER 9

REAL WEALTH

Making the Most Important Decision of Your Life

Every day, think as you wake up, "Today I am fortunate to be
alive, I have a precious human life, I am not going to waste it."
—THE DALAI LAMA

If this book helps you to become financially free, I'll be thrilled for you. But if I'm honest, I don't believe that's *enough*. Why not? Because having financial wealth doesn't guarantee that you'll be wealthy as a human being.

Anybody can make money. As you've learned in the previous chapters, the tools and principles you need are really pretty simple. For example, if you harness the power of compounding, stay in the market for the long term, diversify intelligently, and keep your expenses and taxes as low as possible, your odds of attaining financial freedom are extremely high.

But what if you achieve financial freedom and you're *still* not happy? Many people dream for decades of becoming millionaires or billionaires. Then, when they finally reach their goal, they say: "Is that it? Is that all there is?" And believe me, if you get what you want and you're *still* miserable, then you're really screwed!

When people dream of becoming rich, they're not fantasizing about owning millions of pieces of paper with pictures of dead people on them! What we really want are the *emotions* we associate with money: for example, the sense of freedom, security, or comfort we believe money will give us, or the joy that comes from sharing our wealth. In other words, it's the *feelings* we're after, not the money itself.

I'm not belittling the importance of money. If you use it well, there are countless ways in which it can enrich your life and the lives of those you love. But *real wealth* is about so much more than money. **Real wealth is emotional, psychological, and spiritual.** If you're financially free, but you're still suffering emotionally, then what kind of victory is that?

Maybe this strikes you as an odd digression in a book about money and investing! But I'd feel remiss if I wrote an entire book that shows you how to achieve *financial* wealth while neglecting to share with you the secret of how to achieve *emotional* wealth. Fortunately, you don't have to choose between them! As you'll discover in this chapter, it's possible to be financially rich *and* emotionally rich. This, my friend, is the ultimate prize!

To my mind, the chapter you're about to read is undoubtedly the most important in this book. Why? Because what you'll learn in the pages to come is that there is a *single decision* you can make today that can change the rest of your life. This one decision—if you consistently act on it—will bring you more *joy*, more *peace of mind*, more *real wealth* than most people can imagine. Best of all, you don't need to wait 10, 20, or 30 years. If you make this one decision, you can be rich right *now*!

The truth is, I want to share this idea with you because it's been life changing for me. So, if you're ready to join me, let's begin the final step in our journey!

AN EXTRAORDINARY QUALITY OF LIFE

My entire life has been focused on helping people turn their dreams into reality. I've visited more than 100 countries and have spoken with people from every corner of the earth about what they really want. And do you know what I've found? Every culture has different beliefs and values, yet there are fundamental needs and desires that all human beings share. **What I've found wherever I go is that we all crave *an extraordinary quality of life*.**

For some people, that means owning a beautiful home with an exquisite garden. For others, it means raising three wonderful children. For some, it means writing a novel or a song. For others, it means building a billion-dollar business. And for some, it means being one with God. In other words, it's not about living somebody else's dream. **It's about living a magnificent life on your own terms.**

But how can you achieve this? How can you close the gap between where you are today and where you want to be? The answer: you need to master two entirely different skills.

The Science of Achievement

The first is what I call the "science of achievement." In every field, there are rules of success that you can either break (in which case, you'll be punished) or follow (in which case, you'll be rewarded). For example, there's a science to health and fitness. Biochemically, we're all different. But there are fundamental rules you can follow if you want to thrive and have high energy. If you violate those rules, you'll pay the consequences.

It's the same in the financial world. Just think about what you've learned in this book. The most successful investors have left a trail of clues for us to follow. By studying these patterns and applying these tools, strategies, and principles in your own life, you're accelerating your journey to success. It's obvious, right? Sow the same seeds as the most successful people, and you'll reap the same rewards. That's how you'll achieve financial mastery.

When it comes to the science of achievement, there are three key steps that can enable you to achieve whatever it is you want. Can you think of something fantastic that you've achieved in your life that once seemed impossible? Maybe it was a relationship, or maybe it was a dream job or a successful business, or owning a sleek sports car. Then think about how this dream went from being impossible to actually being in your life. What you'll find is that the path to achievement is followed by a fundamental three-step process.

The First Step to Achieving Anything You Want Is *Focus*. Remember: wherever your focus goes, your energy flows. When you put your entire focus on something that really matters to you, when you can't stop thinking about it every day, this intense focus unleashes a burning desire that can help you obtain what might otherwise be out of reach. Here's what's going on beneath the surface: a part of your brain called the reticular activating system is activated by your desire, and this mechanism draws your attention to whatever can help you achieve your goal.

The Second Step Is to Go Beyond Hunger, Drive, and Desire, and to Consistently Take *Massive Action*. A lot of people dream big but never get started! To succeed, you need to take massive action. But you also need to find the most effective execution strategy, which means changing your approach until you find what works best. You can speed up this process exponentially by modeling people who've already been successful, which is why we've focused so intently on money masters such as Warren Buffett, Ray Dalio, Jack Bogle, and David Swensen. By studying the right role models, you could learn in a week what might otherwise take you a decade.

The Third Step to Achieving Whatever We Want Is Grace. Some people call it luck, some people call it God. Here's what I can tell you, based on my own experience: the more you acknowledge grace in your life, the more you seem to have it! I've been amazed to see how a deep sense of appreciation brings more and more grace into our lives.

Of course, you need to do everything in your power to achieve your goals, but there are still things over which you have no control. Even the fact that you were born at this time in history, that you were given a brain and a heart that you didn't have to earn, and that you get to benefit from the awesome power of modern technologies like the Internet—none of this was within your control, nor did you create these gifts!

Now you know the three basic keys to achievement. **But as important as achievement is, there's a second skill that you'll also need to master if you want to create an extraordinary life. This skill is what I call "the art of fulfillment."**

The Art of Fulfillment

For decades, I was focused obsessively on the science of achievement—on learning to master the external world and on figuring out ways to help people break through and solve every challenge. **But I now believe in my heart and soul that the art of fulfillment is an even more important skill to master. Why? Because if you master the *external world* without mastering the *internal world*, how can you be truly and sustainably happy? That's why my greatest obsession today is the art of fulfillment.**

The $86.9 Million Painting

As I mentioned earlier, we each have a different idea of what constitutes an extraordinary quality of life. To put this another way, what fulfills you is likely to be different from what fulfills me or anyone else. Our needs and desires are infinitely and marvelously diverse! One experience that brought this home to me was an unforgettable day that I spent with a dear friend of mine.

A few years ago, I received a call on his birthday to see where I was. As luck would have it, we were both staying in our vacation homes in Sun Valley, Idaho. So he invited me over to hang out. "When you get here, I've got to show you this painting," he said. "I've coveted it for more than a decade, and I outbid everyone at Sotheby's two days ago and finally bought it! It cost me $86.9 million!"

Can you imagine how intrigued I was to behold this precious treasure that my friend had dreamed of for so long? I was imagining some sort of Renaissance masterpiece that you might see in a museum in Paris or London. But when I got to his house, you know what I found? A painting of a big orange square! I couldn't believe it. I took one look at it and jokingly said, "Give me a hundred bucks' worth of paint, and I can duplicate this in an hour!" He wasn't overly amused. Apparently, this was one of the greatest paintings by the abstract artist Mark Rothko.

So why am I telling you this story? Because it perfectly illustrates the fact that we're all fulfilled by different things. Clearly my friend is more sophisticated than I am when it comes to art, so he could detect a depth of beauty, emotion, and meaning in those brush strokes that I couldn't see. To put it another way, one man's orange splotch is another man's $86.9 million fantasy!

While it's true that we're all different, there are still common patterns when it comes to achieving fulfillment. If that's your goal, what principles or patterns of behavior can you model?

The First Principle: You Must Keep Growing. Everything in life either grows or dies. That goes for relationships, businesses, or anything else. If you *don't* keep growing, you'll become frustrated and miserable, no matter how many millions you have in the bank. In fact, I can tell you the secret to happiness in one word: progress.

The Second Principle: You Have to Give. If you *don't* give, there's only so much you can feel inside, and you'll never feel fully alive. As Winston Churchill said, "You make a living by what you get. You make a life by what you give." Whenever I ask people about the most fulfilling aspects of their lives, they always talk about sharing with others. The true nature of human beings isn't selfish. **We're driven by our desire to contribute. If we stop feeling that deep sense of contribution, we can never feel truly fulfilled.**

It's also worth reminding ourselves of the obvious truth that becoming financially rich is *not* the key to fulfillment. As you and I both know, people often chase after money in the delusional belief that it's a kind of magic potion that will bring joy, meaning, and value to their lives. But money alone will never give you an extraordinary life. Over the years, I've spent a lot of time with billionaires, and some of them are so miserable that you'd feel sorry for them. If you're not happy, you can't have a magnificent life, no matter how fat your wallet.

Remember: money doesn't change people. It just magnifies who they already are: if you have a lot of money and you're mean, then you have more to be mean with; if you have a lot of money and you're generous, you'll naturally give more.

What about professional success? Well, it's wonderful if your success brings you that sense of growth and contribution that we all need in order to feel fulfilled. But I'm sure you've met plenty of "successful" people who never seem happy or fulfilled. And how does *that* qualify as success? **In fact, I truly believe that success without fulfillment is the ultimate failure.**

Let's think for a moment about a painful example of this.

A National Treasure

In 2014 we lost someone whom I consider a national treasure: the actor and comedian Robin Williams. Over the last couple of years, I've spoken to audiences all over the world about this astonishingly gifted man. Again and again, I'd ask the same question: "How many of you in this room loved Robin Williams? Don't raise your hand if you *liked* him—only if you *loved* him." And you know what? Every place I go—from London to Lima, from Tokyo to Toronto—about 98% of the people in the audience raise their hands.

Was Robin Williams a master achiever? Absolutely. He started out with nothing. But then he decides that he wants to star in his own TV show, and he does it. Then he decides that he wants a beautiful family, and he creates it. Then he decides that he wants more money than he can spend in a lifetime, and he makes it happen. Then he decides to become a movie star, and he does it. Then he decides that he wants to win an Oscar—but not for being funny—and he does that, too! Here was a man who had it all, who achieved everything he'd ever dreamed of achieving.

And then he hanged himself.

He hanged himself in his own home, leaving behind hundreds of millions of people who love him to this day. Even more devastating, he left his wife and children traumatized and brokenhearted.

When I think about this terrible tragedy, I'm struck by one simple lesson: if you're not fulfilled, you have nothing.

Robin Williams achieved so much that our culture has conditioned us to value, including fame and fortune. Yet despite all his gifts, it was never enough. He suffered for decades, trying to deal with his stress through the use and sometimes the abuse of alcohol and drugs. Near the end of his life, he was also diagnosed with a progressive neurological disorder, Lewy body disease. His wife, Susan, recently wrote in the medical journal *Neurology*: "Robin was losing his mind, and he was aware of it. Can you imagine the pain he felt as he experienced himself disintegrating?"[18]

Robin Williams was a good man who cared deeply about others—a man who contributed so much to the world, despite his long battle with addiction, depression, and ill health. But in the end, he made everyone happy except himself.

This reminds me of the safety instructions they announce whenever you get on an airplane: "In the event of an emergency, please put on your oxygen

---

18 "By wintertime, problems with paranoia, delusions and looping, insomnia, memory, and high cortisol levels—just to name a few—were settling in hard. Psychotherapy and other medical help was becoming a constant in trying to manage and solve these seemingly disparate conditions," http://www.neurology.org/content/87/13/1308.full.

mask before assisting others." It sounds callous and selfish when you first hear it, but it actually makes sense: unless you help yourself first, how can you hope to help others?

Believe me, I know that Robin Williams is an extreme example. I'm not worried that you're going to kill yourself. But I see so many people—even the "richest" and most "successful" people—who are missing out on so much of the joy and fulfillment they deserve to experience. I want you to experience that joy and fulfillment today. Yet nobody teaches us how to be happy.

To Suffer or Not to Suffer—That Is the Question

A man is but the product of his thoughts. What he thinks, he becomes.
—MAHATMA GANDHI

Let me tell you the story of what's changed in my own life. Over the last two years, I've been on a marvelous journey of the mind. I'm always looking to grow personally, so I'm constantly exploring different ideas about how to reach a whole new level.

A couple of years ago, I was in India visiting a dear friend of mine, Krishnaji, who is equally fascinated by these questions about how to achieve an extraordinary quality of life. As my friend knows, I've taught for many years about the power of being in an "energy-rich" state: a peak state where you can accomplish anything and where your relationships are filled with passion. By contrast, when you're in an "energy-poor" state, the body feels lazy, the mind feels sluggish, and you can't do anything much but worry, get frustrated, and snap at people!

My friend said to me, "What if you use different words to describe these two states?" As he explained, there are really only two different states you can be in at any given moment. Either you're in a high-energy state that could also be described as a "beautiful state." Or you're in a low-energy state (often characterized by internal pain) that could also be described as a "suffering state." He told me that his spiritual vision was to live in a beautiful state no matter what happened in his life.

My friend then echoed what I and so many others have taught for years: We can't control all the events in our lives, but we can control what those events mean to us—and thus what we feel and experience every day of our lives! By consciously choosing and committing to live in a beautiful state, my friend believed that he could not only enjoy so much more of life, but also give so much more to his wife, his child, and to the world at large.

I thought a lot about what he'd said. Now, I'm an achiever. If you're reading this book, you probably are, too. And we achievers don't believe that we're ever "suffering," do we? No! We just have "stress"!

In fact, if you'd told me even two years ago that I was suffering, I would have laughed at you. I have a heavenly wife, four glorious children, total financial freedom, and a mission that inspires me every day of my life. But then I started to realize that I frequently allowed myself to fall into a suffering state. For example, I'd get frustrated, pissed off, overwhelmed, worried, or stressed. At first I figured that those emotions were just a part of life. The truth is, I even convinced myself that I needed them as fuel to move me forward. But this was just my mind playing tricks on me!

The trouble is, the human brain isn't designed to make us happy and fulfilled. It's designed to make us survive. This two-million-year-old organ is always looking for what's wrong, for whatever can hurt us, so that we can either fight it or take flight from it. If you and I leave this ancient survival software to run the show, what chance do we have of enjoying life?

An undirected mind operates naturally in survival mode, constantly identifying and magnifying these potential threats to our well-being. The result: a life filled with stress and anxiety. Most people live this way, since it's the path of least resistance. They make unconscious decisions, based on habit and conditioning, and are at the mercy of their own minds. They assume that it's just an inevitable part of life to get frustrated, stressed, sad, and angry—in other words, to live in a suffering state.

But I'm happy to tell you there's another path: one that involves directing your thoughts so that your mind does your bidding, not the other way around.

This was the path I chose. I decided that I would no longer live in a suffering state. I decided that I would do *everything* in my power to live in a beautiful state for the rest of my life and to become an example of what's humanly possible! After all, there's nothing worse than a rich and privileged man or woman who's angry and ungrateful!

Flying High and Falling Low

Now, before we go any further, let's just clarify the difference between these two emotional and mental states:

A Beautiful State. When you feel love, joy, gratitude, awe, playfulness, ease, creativity, drive, caring, growth, curiosity, or appreciation, you're in a beautiful state. In this state, you know exactly what to do, and you do the right thing. In this state, your spirit and your heart are alive, and the best of you comes out. Nothing feels like a problem, and everything flows. You feel no fear or frustration. You're in harmony with your true essence.

A Suffering State. When you're feeling stressed out, worried, frustrated, angry, depressed, irritable, overwhelmed, resentful, or fearful, you're in a suffering state. We've all experienced these and countless other "negative" emotions, even if we're not always keen to admit it! As I mentioned earlier, most achievers much prefer to think they're stressed than fearful. But "stress" is just the achiever word for fear! If I follow the trail of your stress, it'll take me to your deepest fear.

So what determines whether you're in a beautiful state or a suffering state? You might assume that it depends mostly on your external circumstances. If you're relaxing on a beach and eating ice cream, it's easy to be in a beautiful state! **But in reality, the mental and emotional state in which you live is ultimately the result of where you choose to focus your thoughts.**

I'll give you an example from my own life. For the last 25 years, I've flown back and forth between America and Australia several times a year. Nowadays I'm privileged to have my own plane, which is a bit like having a high-speed office in the sky. For better or for worse, there's no need ever to disconnect from work! But I vividly remember the dread I used to experience when I'd sit down on a commercial flight to Australia and wonder how I could possibly live without connection to emails and texts for the next 14 hours! How could my businesses possibly survive without me?

Then, one magical day, I was sitting on a Qantas Airways flight to Sydney when the captain proudly announced that the plane had international

Internet access. All around me, people started cheering, clapping, and high-fiving one another! It was as if God had descended from on high and entered the plane! I didn't stand up and do a jig, but I have to confess: in my mind, I was clapping, too. And then, after 15 minutes of giddy delight, do you know what happened? We lost Internet access. It didn't work for the rest of the flight, and it's probably *still* not working after all these years.

So how do you think the passengers reacted? We were crushed! One minute, we're euphoric. The next minute, we're cursing our terrible misfortune. What's amazing is how quickly our perspective changed: moments earlier, Internet access had been a miracle; now it was an expectation! All we could think about was that the airline had violated our inalienable right to Internet access—a right that hadn't existed until that very day.

In our outrage, we instantly lost sight of the wonder that we were flying through the air like a bird, crossing the globe in a matter of hours, and watching movies or sleeping as we flew!

Isn't it ridiculous how jaded we are and how upset we allow ourselves to become? When it rains on our parade, when we don't get what we want or expect, we're so quick to give up our happiness and sink into a state of suffering.

Everyone has his or her own flavor of suffering. So here's my question for you: What's *your* favorite flavor of suffering? Which energy-sapping emotion do you indulge in most? Is it sadness? Frustration? Anger? Despair? Self-pity? Jealousy? Worry? The specific details don't really matter because they're *all* states of suffering. **And all this suffering is really just the result of an undirected mind that's hell-bent on looking for problems!**

Think for a moment about a recent situation that caused you pain or suffering—a time when you felt frustrated or angry or worried or overwhelmed. Whenever you feel emotions like these, your sense of suffering is caused by your undirected mind engaging in one or more of three particular patterns of perception. Consciously or unconsciously, you're focused on at least one of three triggers for suffering:

1. Suffering trigger is "Loss." When you focus on loss, you become convinced that a particular problem *has* caused or *will* cause you to lose something you value. For example, you have a conflict with your spouse, and it leaves you feeling that you've lost love or respect. But it doesn't have to be something someone *else* did—or failed to do—that caused you to perceive the sense of loss. This sense of loss can also be triggered by something *you* did or failed to do. For example, you procrastinated, and now you've lost a business opportunity. Whenever we believe in the illusion of loss, we suffer.

2. Suffering trigger is "Less." When you focus on the idea that you *have* less or *will* have less, you will suffer. For example, you might become convinced that because a situation has occurred or a person has acted a certain way, you will have less joy, less money, less success, or some other painful consequence. Once again, less can be triggered by what you, or others, do or fail to do.

3. Suffering trigger is "Never." When you focus on the idea or become consumed by a belief that you'll *never* have something you value—such as love, joy, respect, wealth, opportunity—you're doomed to suffer, you'll never be happy, you'll never become the person you want to be. This pattern of perception is a surefire route to pain. **Remember: the mind is always trying to trick us into a survival mindset! So never say never!** For example, because of an illness, an injury, or because of something your brother did or said, you might believe that you'll never get over it.

These three patterns of focus account for most, if not all, of our suffering. And you know what's crazy? It doesn't even matter if the problem is real or not! Whatever we focus on, we *feel*—regardless of what actually happened. Have you ever had the experience of thinking that a friend did something horrible to you? You became tremendously angry and upset, only to discover that you were dead wrong and that the person didn't deserve all that blame! In the midst of your suffering, when all those negative emotions were swirling inside your head, the reality didn't matter. Your focus created your feelings, and your feelings created your experience. Notice, too, that most, if not all, of our suffering is caused by focusing or obsessing about ourselves and what we might lose, have less of, or never have.

But here's the good news: once you're aware of these patterns of focus, you can systematically change them, thereby freeing yourself from these habits of suffering. It all starts with the realization that this involves a conscious choice. **Either you master your mind or it masters you. The secret of living an extraordinary life is to take control of the mind, since this alone will determine whether you live in a suffering state or a beautiful state.**

IN THE END, IT'S ALL ABOUT THE POWER OF DECISIONS

Our lives are shaped not by our conditions, but by our decisions. If you look back on the last 5 or 10 years I'd be willing to bet that you can recall a decision or two that has truly changed your life. Maybe it was a decision about where to go to school, what profession to pursue, or who you chose to love or marry. Looking back on it now, can you see how radically different your life would be today if you had made a different decision? These and so many other decisions determine the direction of your life and can change your destiny.

So what's the biggest decision you can make in your life right now? In the past, I would have told you that what matters most is who you decide to spend your time with, who you decide to love. After all, the company you keep will powerfully shape who you become.

But over the last two years, my thinking has evolved. **What I've come to realize is that the single most important decision in life is this:** *Are you committed to being happy, no matter what happens to you?*

To put this another way, will you commit to enjoying life not only when everything goes your way but also when everything goes against you, when injustice happens, when someone screws you over, when you lose something or someone you love, or when nobody seems to understand or appreciate you? Unless we make this definitive decision to stop suffering and live in a beautiful state, our survival minds will create suffering whenever our desires, expectations, or preferences are not met. What a waste of so much of our lives!

This is a decision that can change everything in your life, starting today. But it's not enough just to say that you'd *like* to make this change or that your *preference* is to be happy no matter what. You have to own this decision, do whatever it takes to make it happen, and cut off any possibility of turning back. **If you want to take the island, you have to burn the boats. You**

**have to decide that you're 100% responsible for your state of mind and
for your experience of this life.**

What it really comes down to is drawing a line in the sand today and
declaring, **"I'm done with suffering. I'm going to live every day to the
fullest and find juice in every moment, including the ones I don't like,
BECAUSE LIFE IS JUST TOO SHORT TO SUFFER."**

BEWARE OF GODZILLA!

There are many different techniques you can use to take control of your
mind and achieve a beautiful state. This is such an important subject that
I plan to write an entire book about it. But you don't need to wait to begin
this life-changing journey. You can decide right now that you will no longer
settle for a life that's less than the one you deserve to feel and experience. All
you have to do to change your life forever is commit in your heart and soul
to find something to appreciate in every moment. Then you will experience
the real wealth of ongoing happiness!

Are you up for making this bold and brilliant decision right now?! If so,
let's support you by reviewing two simple techniques that I've found enormously helpful in staying on this course.

The first tool is what I call "the 90-second rule." Whenever I start to
suffer, I give myself 90 seconds to stop it so that I can return to living in a
beautiful state. Sounds good, right? But how do you actually *do* it?

Let's say I'm having an intense conversation with an employee at one of
my companies and discover that he or she has made a mistake that could
cause an array of problems. Naturally, my brain leaps into danger detec-
tion mode, launches that ancient survival software, and starts bombarding
me with thoughts about all the ways I and our whole team might suffer as a
result. In the past, I could have easily been swept up in a whirlwind of worry,
frustration, or anger—a maelstrom of mental suffering!

But here's what I do now. As soon as I feel the tension rising in my body,
I catch myself. **And the way that I catch myself is really simple: I gently
breathe and slow things down. I step out of the situation and start
to distance myself from all those stressful thoughts that my brain is
generating.**

It's natural for these thoughts to arise, but they're just thoughts. When you slow down, you realize that you **don't have to believe these thoughts or identify with them.** You can step back and say to yourself, "Wow, look at that crazy thought go by! There goes that crazy mind again!" Why is this helpful? Because the problem isn't the *existence* of our negative, destructive, and limiting thoughts—everyone has those! What hurts us is the habit of *believing* those thoughts. For example, have you ever found yourself getting so mad at someone that you started to think, "Man, I really want to throttle this guy! I could kill him!" I'm guessing that you didn't actually do it. Why? Because you didn't believe the thought. At least, I hope you didn't!

Once I've detached myself from these unwanted thoughts, I start to focus my mind on finding something to appreciate. The survival brain is always searching for what's wrong, but there's always something to appreciate. As I always say, **"What's wrong is always available . . . but so is what's right!"** Maybe it's the simple fact that I'm alive and well, that I'm still breathing! Maybe it's the fact that the person who made the mistake is a beautiful human being who works hard and has the best intentions. Maybe it's the fact that I have the awareness to see that I'm suffering, which gives me the ability to stop and let it go immediately.

It doesn't matter *what* you appreciate. What matters is that by shifting your focus to appreciation, you slow down your survival mechanism. Love, joy, and giving, will all trigger the same positive transformation. This shift in your focus creates space for your spirit to enter the game, so you don't get stuck inside your head. If you keep doing this with real consistency, you actually rewire your nervous system, training your mind to find the good in every situation, so your experience of life is one of thankfulness and joy.

And you know what's miraculous? Before you know it, you feel free. You let go and start to laugh at things that used to drive you nuts. This makes for a happier life and healthier relationships, while also helping you to think more clearly and make smarter decisions. After all, when you're stressed, angry, sad, or fearful, you're not likely to find the best solutions. When you're in a beautiful state, the answers come more easily. It's like tuning a radio to the right frequency so the static disappears and you can hear the music loud and clear.

When I first began to use this technique, I should have called it the four-hour rule or the four-day rule because it sometimes took me so long to stop suffering and regain my equilibrium! **But it's like any skill: the more you use it, the better you get.** I've found that it really helps when I catch myself quickly, instead of letting those negative thoughts linger for longer than 90 seconds. Why? Because the best time to kill any monster is when it's little. You don't want to wait until it's Godzilla and it's devouring your entire city!

I'm still not perfect at this, and there are certainly times when I get hooked. But I use the 90-second rule so often that it's gone from being a discipline to becoming a habit. This one technique has given me an amazing level of freedom from all those destructive emotions that used to rob me of my joy and peace of mind. Those emotions still come, but they disappear quickly, overwhelmed by the power of appreciation and enjoyment. As a result, life is more beautiful than ever!

What you'll also find is that you're much more present for other people when you're not caught up in your own thoughts of *loss*, *less*, and *never*. When you're in a beautiful state, you can give so much more to everyone you love.

And you know what? There's power in happiness. There's a happiness advantage in life. Happiness is an advantage in your relationships, your business, your health, and in everything you touch. Living in a beautiful state no matter what is the ultimate freedom **and the ultimate gift that you can give to those you love. It's the experience of absolute abundance—and abundance of joy!—that is true wealth.**

Even better, you can possess this abundance now, instead of having to wait until you acquire a certain amount of money! And the good news is, this decision rests entirely in your hands. You alone can give yourself this happiness edge.

UNCHAIN YOUR HEART: THE POWER OF ALIGNMENT!

To overcome fear, the best thing is to be overwhelmingly grateful.
—SIR JOHN TEMPLETON

The second tool I'd like to share with you is a simple two-minute gratitude meditation that I've taught to tens of thousands of people in my seminars over the last year or so. I've recorded this meditation and made it available online at www.unshakeable.com and on the Unshakeable mobile app, so you can listen to the audio with your eyes closed.

But I'm also giving you a written version below. We all absorb information in different ways. So you may prefer to read this over, get a general sense of the instructions, and then do this brief meditation from memory, without the audio. I've found that reading it once to understand where the process is going is valuable, but it's much easier to listen to it, so you can stay out of the mind and in your heart. Either way, I hope you'll discover that it's a powerful technique for aligning your mind and your heart, quickly placing you in a beautiful state.

But first, let me give you a quick word of explanation about the science behind this meditation. If you went to a hospital and we hooked you up to an electroencephalogram (EEG) and an electrocardiogram (EKG), we could measure the electrical impulses in your brain and in your heart. What you'd see when you're stressed out and suffering mentally is that the lines on the EEG and the EKG would look jagged. But the jaggedness from your *heart's*

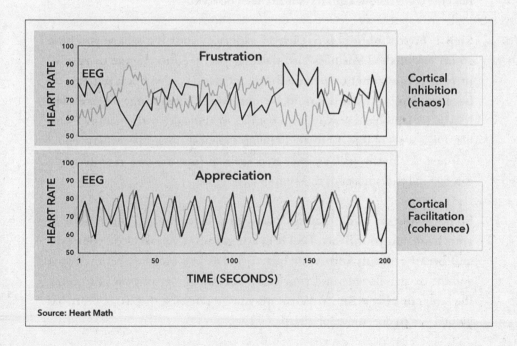

rhythms would look nothing like the jaggedness from your *brain*'s rhythms. In other words, they're out of sync.

But scientific studies have shown that this short meditative focus can dramatically alter those electrical impulses in your brain and your heart. What's miraculous is that the jagged lines on the EEG and the EKG tend to become rounded after this meditation. What's more, the lines from the heart and the brain become almost identical. Why? Because the mind and the heart are now operating as one. This is what happens naturally when you're in a state of flow.

The simple goal of this meditation is to change your emotional state by filling you with a sense of gratitude, and to use that emotion to solve whatever challenge has been causing you to suffer. Why gratitude? Because you can't be grateful and angry at the same time. You can't be grateful and fearful at the same time. If you want a miserable life, there's no better way to achieve it than to focus your mind on anger and fear! But if you want a happy life, if you want to live in a beautiful state, nothing works better than to focus on gratitude!

So if you're ready to test-drive this technique, go to the audio now or read the steps below. Here's what I'd like you to do:

Step 1. First, I want you to pick an aspect of your life where you have some "unfinished business": something you need to change or resolve in your professional or personal life; an issue you've been putting off because dealing with it would be upsetting, frustrating, or stressful. Maybe it's a problem at work or a conflict or difficulty with a family member. On a scale of 0 to 10 (with 10 being the most upsetting), where would you rank it? Ideally, pick an issue that ranks at least a 6 or a 7, so that you can feel the true impact of this simple technique.

Step 2. Now set aside that situation for a moment and place both of your hands on your heart. Feel it beating. I want you to close your eyes and breathe deeply into your heart. And as you breathe, feel the blood and the oxygen flowing into your heart. Feel the power of your heart. Find the strength of your heart. What are you grateful for that your heart has guided you to do, enjoy, appreciate, or give?

Step 3. As you breathe deeply, feel grateful for your heart. Feel what a gift your heart is. Every day it beats a hundred thousand times and pumps blood through 60 thousand miles of blood vessels. You don't even have to think about your heart, and yet it's always there for you, even while you sleep. It's the ultimate gift, and yet you didn't have to earn it. It was given to you. Something loved you so much that it gave you this heart. And as long as it beats in your chest, you live. What a gift! Feel the power of that gift now.

Step 4. As you breathe into your heart, feeling deep gratitude for your heart, I want you to physically feel your heartbeat. And as you're doing this, I want you to think of three experiences in your life for which you feel incredibly grateful—and you're going to step into those three experiences one at a time. They could be big or small. They could date back to your childhood, or they could be from this week or even today.

Step 5. I want you to think of the first experience and step into it right now as if you're there, inside that memory, reliving it. See what you saw in that moment of pure gratitude: feel it, breathe it, own it, and feel so grateful for that moment. Fill yourself up with gratitude because when you're grateful, there is no sadness, there is no hurt, there is no anger. You can't be grateful and angry simultaneously. You can't be grateful and worried simultaneously. If we cultivate gratitude, we have a different life.

   Now think of a second experience, another moment for which you can feel so grateful—something that felt like a pure gift in your life, a miracle, an act of grace, of love. And fill yourself up with the beauty and the joy of that experience. Fill yourself up with deep gratitude for that moment, taking time to feel it and appreciate it fully for at least 30 seconds.

   Next, I want you to think of a third moment for which you could feel so grateful. But don't just think about it. Step into that experience, step into that environment, and feel what you felt in that moment. Savor it. Fill yourself up with the joy, the miracle, the gift of that experience.

Step 6. And now I want you to think of one more experience, but this time I want it to be an experience that was a coincidence. It wasn't something you'd planned for, and yet it brought such joy into your life.

Maybe that chance experience led to your meeting a person you love or who changed your life or who enriched your life. Or maybe it led to a new career choice, or brought you new opportunities for growth or happiness. This coincidence happened just for you. Was it a coincidence, or were you guided?

I have a core belief that has often pulled me out of pain and into meaning. **In my soul, I believe that life is always happening for us, not to us!** Even the most painful situations cause us to grow, to expand, to deepen, or to care more. I'm sure there have been events in your life that you'd never want to go through again. Yet when you look back on it 5 or 10 years later, you see the higher purpose in it all. You see how life was actually working for you in that moment. Even those moments of suffering turned out to be great triggers for growth.

Take a moment to give thanks to whatever you believe has given you these gifts. Fill yourself up with gratitude to the universe or God or whatever you believe in. And trust in this universe, which is billions of years old, and which has always taken care of you, even when you felt that you'd lost your way!

Step 7. And now, as you breathe into your heart and feel this tremendous gratitude, I want you to remember the issue that was upsetting you earlier. As you stay in this beautiful state, feeling filled with gratitude, I want you to ask yourself a simple question: "All I need to remember about that situation, all I need to focus on, all I need to believe, all I need to do is . . . what?"

Don't filter. Your first, instinctive heartfelt thoughts are usually the right ones. As you remain in this beautiful state, ask yourself that question again: "All I need to remember about that situation, all I need to focus on, all I need to believe, all I need to do is . . . what?"

And your heart knows the answer, doesn't it? Yes, it does. Trust your heart. It knows what to do. Breathe into your heart and give thanks for the answer. Your heart and mind aligned are a powerful force. When unified, they're unbeatable.

It's much easier to listen to this meditation than to read it, so please take advantage of the app audio. As I mentioned earlier, I've guided tens of thousands of people through this meditation. At this point, I ask them to raise a hand if they know what to do in this situation that used to stress them out. I then ask them to open their eyes and look around the room to see how many people have raised their hands. It's usually about 95% of the audience. In some cases, the situation requires more intense work. But this simple 2-minute meditation is just one of many techniques I can use to help them.

But here's the broader point I'm making: you and I have the power to vault ourselves out of a suffering state and into a beautiful state in just two minutes. How? By focusing on what we appreciate. **It's so simple and yet so profound: appreciation, enjoyment, and love are nothing less than the antidotes to suffering. It's all about shifting your focus away from the illusion of loss, less, or never, and engaging your gratitude, appreciation, and love for what you already have in your life!**

Take all of your negative thoughts and all of your negative emotions, trade them for appreciation, and your whole life changes in an instant.

A DREAM OF HAPPINESS AND A VISION OF HOPE

Yesterday is but a dream,
And tomorrow is only a vision.
But today well lived makes every yesterday
a dream of happiness,
And every tomorrow a vision of hope.
—KĀLIDĀSA, Sanskrit dramatist and poet, ca. fifth century CE

Now, I'm not saying that you'll never suffer or be stressed again. You know as well as I do that life is full of extreme circumstances. No matter how smart we are or how rich we are, none of us is immune to health issues, the pain of losing people we love, and a myriad of other difficulties.

I can't control what's going to happen to you or your family in the future. I can't control what will happen with the financial markets, including the possibility of a crash that lasts longer and is more severe than anyone

expects. I wish I could . . . **But I promise you this: if you make the decision to master your own mind, you'll be mentally equipped to handle
whatever challenges come your way.**

Some people are experts on posttraumatic stress. But I've spent a lifetime
focusing on the miracle of posttraumatic *growth*. I study resilient people
who've been through the worst situations and *still* end up creating magnificent lives.

A few years ago, I met an incredible woman named Alice Herz-Sommer,
a brilliant pianist born in Czechoslovakia in 1903. During World War II,
Alice and her son were deported and sent to a concentration camp. She was
forced to give piano recitals in the camp—and somehow pretend that she
was gladly performing for her Nazi captors. Otherwise they would have
killed her child. The extraordinary story of how Alice survived these experiences with her spirit intact is recounted in a biography entitled *A Garden of
Eden in Hell*.

When I met Alice, she was 108 years old and living in England. She had
endured so much tragedy, yet she was one of the most positive and inspiring
people I've ever encountered, full of life and joy. She lived on her own and
insisted on taking care of herself. She still played piano and sang every day.
What struck me most was that everything seemed beautiful to her.

How amazing is that? To me, it's the ultimate reminder that even someone who has been through hell can be filled with happiness. I was most

deeply moved by her description of her time in the concentration camp. Alice told me that every moment of her life—including those years—had been a gift.

When you meet people like this, you never forget them because they possess such an outstanding ability to live in appreciation, awe, and gratitude. Despite all of their challenges, they radiate love and joy. And then there are those people you want to slap in the head because they freak out when the milk in their caffè latte isn't hot enough!

So what are you going to do? Are you going to join me in my quest to experience true and lasting wealth today by training your mind to find joy in every moment? It's your choice whether to live in a suffering state or a beautiful state. You have the capability to become a master of enjoyment, to fill your mind with appreciation, to be happy no matter what. Best of all, the joy in you will affect everyone around you.

If you're ready to burn the boats and take the island, I recommend that you write a note explaining your decision to live in a beautiful state and why you've made it. Then send this note to three people you respect and ask them to tell you (gently!) if they ever see you slipping into a suffering state. You can also send the note to me at **endsufferingnow@tonyrobbins.com**. I'd be touched to hear that you've made this decision, why you made it, and how it's enriched your life.

By writing down your decision, you crystalize it, while also committing yourself publicly in a way that will help you stay the course. Even better, you may well inspire the recipients of your note to follow you in making this commitment to live in a beautiful state.

Everyone needs a vision. Mine is simple. I'm going to live in a beautiful state every day of my life—and when I get off track, I will snap myself back immediately. This will enable me to bring more beauty to the lives of others and all those I love. I hope you'll join me in this mission. Because let me tell you: living in a beautiful state is the greatest prize, the real jackpot, the ultimate treasure. This is rarer—and a much greater achievement—than being a millionaire or billionaire. If you can learn to ride the roller coaster of life and enjoy both the ups and the downs, then you are utterly unshakeable.

THE SECRET TO LIVING IS GIVING

I started this chapter by talking about real wealth. So, as we come to the end of our time together, what is it? And how can you truly experience it every day? **When I interviewed Sir John Templeton, one of the first great international investors to become a billionaire, I asked him, "What's the secret to wealth?"** He said, "Tony, it's what you teach." I laughed and said, "I teach a lot of things. Which thing?"

With a big smile on his face, he replied, "Gratitude! You know, Tony, we've both met people who have a billion dollars and they're miserable. So they're truly poor. And we both know people who seemingly have nothing, yet they're grateful for the breath of life, for everything. So they're rich beyond compare."

In our hearts we all know it's not money that makes us rich. As I'm sure you've found, the greatest treasures are *never* financial. It's those moments of grace when we appreciate the perfection and beauty of it all. It's those moments when we feel something eternal and invincible inside us, the core of our spirit. It's the loving warmth of our relationships with family and friends. It's finding meaningful work. It's the capacity to learn and grow, to share and serve.

For me, it's also the joy of helping people to break through their limits and seeing them light up as they remember who they really are and what they're really capable of achieving. It's the delight of seeing their lives become a celebration instead of a battle. It's the magical feeling that somehow I've made a little difference, that I've played a role in the awakening of a marvelous and unique human being. It's appreciating that everything I've gone through has served not only me but others—that even the deepest pain I've experienced has led to something beautiful. In fact, there can be no greater gift than for your life to have meaning beyond yourself.

This is the ultimate game changer. Find something to serve, a cause you can be passionate about that's greater than yourself, and this will make you wealthy. Nothing enriches us as much as helping others.

People often say they'll give when they're rich. But the truth is, you can start giving even when you have very little. If a person won't give a dime out of a dollar they will never give $100,000 out of $1 million! Start now with whatever you have, and I can promise you blessings beyond compare! This psychological shift from scarcity to abundance makes you wealthy and brings you a glorious sense of freedom. In making this shift, you're training your brain to recognize that there's so much more available for you to give, to appreciate, and to love. And remember: It's not just money that you can donate. You can also give your time, your talent, your love, your compassion, your heart.

My daily prayer is to be a blessing in the lives of all those I meet. If you make the tools and principles in this book a part of your core, you'll be able to receive—and give—more than you could ever imagine. As this extraordinary abundance flows *to* you and *from* you, you will feel truly blessed—and you will become a greater and greater blessing in the lives of others. This is what it feels like to possess real wealth.

I'm thankful that you've allowed me the privilege of spending this time with you. I sincerely hope the contents of this book have been helpful to you on your journey to financial freedom. Perhaps someday our paths will cross, and I'll have the privilege of hearing the story of how this book has helped you accelerate the building of the life you desire and deserve.

Please return to these pages whenever you need a reminder of who you really are and all that you can create. Remember that you are more than the moment. You are more than your economics. You are more than any challenging time you may face. You are soul, spirit, and essence—and you are truly unshakeable. God bless you!

—Tony Robbins

CREATIVE PLANNING

Creative Planning is a nationally recognized leader in the wealth management community focused on providing clients with customized investment plans and comprehensive wealth management services. Our fierce commitment to independence means you get unbiased advice, not sales. No hidden fees, commissions, or proprietary mutual funds to cloud our vision or promote conflicts of interest. We are singularly focused on providing advice and solutions that champion your best interests.

Below are a few of the accolades we have earned over the years:

- number one wealth management firm in the United States (CNBC, 2014, 2015);
- number one independent advisor in America (*Barron's*, 2013, 2014, 2015);
- number one wealth management firm in America (*Barron's*, 2017): and
- number one investment advisor in the United States for ten-year growth (*Forbes*, 2016).

We currently manage $35 billion and growing for clients across all 50 states.
www.getasecondopinion.com

ACKNOWLEDGMENTS

As I look back on some 40 years of this mission, I see the faces of so many extraordinary human beings. Briefly here, I'd like to express my deep gratitude to those who have touched this particular project.

First, my family, of course. This begins and ends with my wife, Bonnie Pearl—my Sage. I love you. I give thanks for the grace that breathes our love and our life. To my entire family and all of our extended family, I love you.

To my friend Peter Mallouk, I'm forever grateful for that fateful conversation you had with me in LA. I couldn't have asked for a more brilliant, honest, and sincere human being for a business partner. Thank you.

To Josh, thanks for going on this journey with me again. Creating and laughing, I've loved every moment of our time together, and I'm so proud of our work. To Ajay Gupta and the entire Creative Planning team and to Tom Zgainer, my sincere gratitude.

To my core team at Robbins Research International—Sam, Yogesh, Scotty, Shari, Brook, Rich, Jay, Katie, Justin, and all the rest of our fiercely loyal and mission-driven executive staff—I count my blessings for you every day. Thanks to Kwaku and to Brittany and Michael. And I couldn't have pulled this book off without my right arm Mary Buckheit and my wickedly smart creative team, especially Diane Adcock. I love you; thank you, ladies.

To Jennifer Connelly, Jan Miller, Larry Hughes, thank you. To all personnel at San Diego HQ and all our partners that make up the Tony Robbins Companies, thank you for all you do in our quest to create breakthroughs in every area of life.

My life has been powerfully shaped by deep friendships with three brilliant men. To my role models Peter Guber, Marc Benioff, and Paul Tudor

Jones, thank you for your love and for being such brilliant, creative, impeccable human beings. To be your friend is such a gift. Each day I spend with you is another day I am inspired to take my game to another level.

Through events and appearances around the world, I am afforded the opportunity to meet hundreds of thousands of gorgeous people each year who touch my life deeply. But this book, at its core, and its predecessor, *MONEY Master the Game*, was uniquely shaped by a group of more than 50 extraordinary souls whose insights and strategies have been massively impactful to me and to all who read these pages. My deepest thanks, respect, and admiration for those who shared their precious time and life's work in our interview sessions. I am eternally grateful. To Ray Dalio, Jack Bogle, Steve Forbes, Alan Greenspan, Mary Callahan Erdoes, John Paulson, Harry Markowitz, and Howard Marks: your wisdom is unrivaled, I am truly inspired by your mastery, and I'm privileged to learn from each one of you. Thank you.

More thanks to T. Boone Pickens, Kyle Bass, Charles Schwab, Sir John Templeton, Carl Icahn, Robert Schiller, Dan Ariely, Burton Malkiel, Alicia Munnell, Teresa Ghilarducci, Jeffrey Brown, David Babbel, Larry Summers, David Swensen, Marc Faber, Warren Buffett, and George W. Bush. Thanks to all those who provided interviews or who gave of their time at my Platinum Partnership Wealth Mastery events, and for those who have shared your insights over the years and who have served as examples of what is possible—you all inspire me, and your insights are echoed in these pages in many ways.

Thanks again to all my partners at Simon & Schuster, namely Jonathan Karp and Ben Loehnen. To William Green for your intelligence and British humor, and most of all, for joining us on this project and for caring so deeply about every last word and em dash. Thanks also to Cindy DiTiberio for your commitment to this manuscript.

Of course, the mission of this book is to serve not only those who will be reading. And so my deepest thanks to everyone at the Anthony Robbins Foundation and our strategic partners, namely Dan Nesbit at Feeding America for helping us coordinate this never-before-attempted approach to provide food to our hungry neighbors. The distribution of my initial donation of one hundred million meals and the efforts of all those working tirelessly to secure matching funds that will enable the delivery of a billion meals over the next 8 years.

To the grace that has guided this entire process, and to all those friends and teachers along the path of my life—too many to mention, some famous and some unknown, whose insights, strategies, example, love, and caring are the shoulders I have had the honor to stand on. On this day, I give thanks to you all, and I continue my never-ending quest to each day be a blessing in the lives of all those I have the privilege to meet, love, and serve.

TONY ROBBINS COMPANIES

Tony Robbins is a global entrepreneur, investor, *New York Times* number one bestselling author, philanthropist, sports team owner, and the world's number one life and business strategist.

LEADER, TEACHER, AND LIFE AND BUSINESS STRATEGIST

Over the last four decades, more than 50 million people from more than 100 countries have enjoyed the warmth, humor, and transformational power of his books, audio and video trainings, and more than 4 million people have attended his live events.

He has coached global leaders and presidents of nations, including Bill Clinton, Mikhail Gorbachev, and Princess Diana. He has helped transform top sports teams, including three NBA title–winning teams, plus individual standouts such as Serena Williams and Andre Agassi. Award-winning actors and entertainers including Leonardo DiCaprio, Hugh Jackman, Anthony Hopkins, and Pitbull also call on him for coaching.

He has coached some of the world's most successful entrepreneurs and billionaire businessmen, including Marc Benioff, CEO and founder of Salesforce.com; Peter Guber, chairman and CEO of Mandalay Entertainment Group, and owner of the Golden State Warriors and Los Angeles Dodgers; and billionaire hotel and gaming mogul Steve Wynn, chairman and CEO of Wynn Resorts & Casinos.

ENTREPRENEURSHIP AND INVESTING

Robbins is a founder of, or partner in, 31 companies, 12 of which he actively manages across seven different industries, with combined annual sales of more than $5 billion. His companies are as diverse as a five-star Fijian island resort (Namale Resort and Spa) and a virtual reality company that is the exclusive partner of the NBA and Live Nation concerts (NextVR). He is also an ownership partner of various sports teams, such as the Los Angeles Football Club (LAFC) and Team Liquid—the leading organization in the world in the growing eSports sector.

PHILANTHROPY

Tony has long been an extraordinary philanthropist who has never forgotten his roots—specifically, the time someone provided a Thanksgiving dinner for *his* family in a time of need when he was just 11 years old. He has provided 350 million meals for hungry families, and over the next 7 years, he will provide a billion meals for those in need through his partnership with Feeding America.

In addition to his mission to feed the hungry, Robbins provides 250,000 people per day with fresh water in India, and is targeting to hit a million people per day over the next 5 years. Robbins has also partnered with Elon Musk and other innovators by providing $1 million of the $15 million XPrize for Education. He has also partnered with Operation Underground Railroad to free more than 1,500 children from sexual slavery.

AWARDS AND ACCOLADES

- *Worth* magazine has twice named him to its Power 100 list of the most influential leaders in global finance.
- He has been honored by Accenture as one of the "top 50 business intellectuals in the world"; by Harvard Business Publishing as one of the "top 200 business gurus"; and by American Express as one of the "top six business leaders in the world" to coach its entrepreneurial clients.
- *Fortune* magazine's cover story called him "the CEO whisperer," for his extraordinary work as the "leader called upon by leaders."

OTHER WORKS BY TONY ROBBINS

BOOKS

MONEY Master the Game: 7 Simple Steps to Financial Freedom

Awaken the Giant Within

Unlimited Power

AUDIO PROGRAMS

The Ultimate Edge: We all want to achieve our vision of an extraordinary life, but most simply don't know how or where to begin. Many lack the strategies, tools, and inner strength to make lasting change and may even have limiting beliefs and obstacles holding them back. The Ultimate Edge can help you in discovering the strength inside you to break through barriers and create massive results. In this powerful 3-part Ultimate Edge audio program, Tony Robbins personally instructs you to connect with what you truly want most and how you can start to achieve it. Tony's life and career has been defined by an obsession with creating change and influencing massive action in people's lives. Now available on the App Store and Google Marketplace.

DOCUMENTARY

Check out the Netflix documentary *Tony Robbins: I Am Not Your Guru*.

For more on Tony Robbins go to www.TonyRobbins.com.

APPENDIX

Your Checklist for Success: Fortifying Your Kingdom—How to Protect Your Assets, Build Your Legacy, and Insure Against the Unknown

Invincibility lies in the defense.
—SUN TZU, *The Art of War*

Congratulations on taking this journey with us. I hope you feel more prepared, informed, and fully equipped to achieve financial freedom after reading this book. As you know now, *Unshakeable* isn't just the title—it's a way of living that can permeate every aspect of your life. Ultimately, it means freedom and peace of mind.

Yet the truth is, none of us has absolute control over the future. There are a variety of unknowns that could emerge to prevent you from enjoying the very wealth you have worked so hard to build.

- What if you are no longer able to work due to an unexpected illness or disability?
- What if you get slapped with a lawsuit, putting all your hard-earned money in jeopardy?
- What happens to your money if you're confronted with the harsh realities of divorce?
- What happens to your wealth and legacy when you inevitably pass away?

Remember how we said that losers react and leaders anticipate? Anticipation can be the ultimate power. And these final pages are all about anticipation—both of things that you *know* will happen and things that you pray will not. I know, I know, it's not the most fun thing to sit down and plan for unlikely events or one's eventual passing. However, there will be tremendous relief and peace of mind once you buckle down and bulletproof your wealth. There's nothing like the unshakeable feeling of knowing that you and those you love will never have to worry about any external events disturbing the quality of your lives.

Remember Ray Dalio's mantra to expect surprises? This section allows you to do just that. For the same reasons that you diversify your portfolio, the items in this checklist allow you to prepare for all those unknowns that could be lurking around the corner. Plus, you'll discover even more ways to save on taxes!

Think of *true* wealth management as the building of your personal financial kingdom. At the center is your portfolio, but you must fortify all the areas in and around the kingdom to protect your treasure from being destroyed or eroded by unnecessary taxes, costly lawsuits, or government intervention. And ultimately you want your heirs to get *exactly* what you wish upon your death, or to be able to leave a legacy of impact and philanthropy to causes of your choice.

We'll keep this section as short as possible. This is not even really a chapter. It's designed to be a guide or checklist. In fact, there are four distinct checklists for you to utilize with your attorney and financial advisor: one for health, one for wealth, one for insurance, and one for charitable giving.

> Dearly beloved / We are gathered here today
> to get through this thing called life
> —PRINCE, "Let's Go Crazy"

In 2016, millions of fans around the world mourned the unexpected loss of the icon we came to know as Prince—one of my favorite artists. According to the *New York Times*, Prince died at 57 years young without a will. He didn't set up an estate plan or take any necessary steps to protect his estimated $300 million estate. Now instead of his assets going to his family, they'll be tied up in court for years, and the government is guaranteed more than $120 million, or 40% of his estate—all because he failed to put together a plan.

While purple may not be your favorite color and you might not win seven Grammys, the lesson is clear. Whether we realize it or not, if we fail to plan, we are planning to fail.

Now, to walk you through these checklists and to make sure you can avoid these missteps that have harmed so many in the past, I'm going to pass the ball to my partner, Peter Mallouk, because, as you know by now, he is one of the top financial advisors in the country according to *Barron's* and CNBC—and an estate-planning attorney to boot! In the pages that follow, he provides you, free of charge(!), the same advice he gives his own clients. So be sure not to miss any of this. Then bring this book to your meeting with your advisors and get your financial world in order.

TRANSFERRING AND PROTECTING YOUR WEALTH WITH PETER MALLOUK

Hold on! Before you put down this book with one of the many excuses I've heard before, let me just address them straight on:

"I Don't Really Have That Much, So It's Not Important to Set Up a Will"

If it's not important, why do you work? Why do you invest? Why do you budget? Of course this is important, and you've probably put this off because it seems like a hassle. It can be done quickly and inexpensively, and your family deserves to be protected, don't they?

"I'm Young, and This Stuff Is Irrelevant to Me"

This is relevant to you if you have people you care about—a mother, a father, a grandfather, an aunt or uncle—who have not taken the time to set up protection for themselves and their family.

"I Have a Lot of Assets, So It's Going to Be a Hassle"

If you think it's going to be a hassle to set up your estate plan now, imagine what it will be like for your loved ones if you become incapacitated or die. I'm sorry to be blunt, but I must nudge you here. If you have significant assets, you should begin your estate planning immediately! There is no time to waste. None of us knows how much time we have left. Putting this off can have catastrophic consequences.

"My Personal Situation Is Complicated"

If you think your situation is complicated and will involve tough decisions (for instance, children from multiple marriages, five ex-spouses, and so on), imagine what it will be like to have your estate go through probate. The probate court, with all the efficiency and effectiveness of a state-run program, will make all of those tough decisions for you without the benefit of your input. (I hope you picked up on my sarcasm.)

"I Don't Even Know What Probate Is. And Why Should I Care? I'll Be Dead!"

Probate is the process that a court uses to establish the validity of a will (if there is one) and recognize the executor. If there is no will, the court will appoint an *administrator* of its choosing to handle the affairs required by probate.

Better the Devil You Know . . .

So let's just admit that the downsides of avoiding the inevitable are more costly than the onetime hassle of meeting with your financial advisor or lawyer. In the four checklists that follow, we'll tackle setting up measures to protect you if you fall ill, we'll discuss your estate plan or will, we'll talk about ways to protect your assets while you're alive, and then, finally, we'll talk about creating a legacy of generosity.

These lists are designed to be used with your advisor of choice. If you don't have a financial advisor, a tax expert, an insurance specialist, and an attorney in your corner, or if you would simply like a second opinion, know that we handle all of these areas as part of our family office services at Creative Planning. If you have any questions or would like our guidance, feel free to reach us at www.getasecondopinion.com.

Checklist 1: I Got the Power

If I am incapacitated, I really don't care who makes health care decisions for me, nor do I care who handles my financial affairs. If a choice has to be made, I think the government is the best choice to do all this for me.
—SAID NO ONE EVER

I had a client who, at 53, despite seeming to be in perfect health, suddenly became unresponsive. As her family rushed her to the hospital, it was soon determined that she had a brain tumor. She had not set up power of attorney, and thus her husband was unable to access any of her accounts and get her disability benefits activated. She passed away shortly thereafter, never having regained consciousness, and the family soon learned that she had not set up her will, leading her estate to go into probate.

The three items on this checklist could have been taken care of with a few simple decisions. This is not complex stuff. Any qualified attorney can quickly handle these core essentials, and these documents would have protected my client's family. Here's what you *must* do, if nothing else, to protect you and yours.

Durable Power of Attorney for Health Care (Health Care Proxy)
What if you or your spouse suddenly become incapacitated and are no longer able to make any decisions on your own? Who is going to make medical decisions about your care should this happen? This is something you should think about now, while you have, yes, the power. If you have a living spouse, he or she might be your first choice. Make sure to consider the implications of the person you choose. (For instance, if you have a lot of life insurance, you might want to give authority to someone who isn't invested in pulling the plug!) Okay, I'm kidding, but all joking aside, you need someone you trust inherently who can make the entire range of decisions, from whether to remove life support as mentioned, or whether to change doctors, or whether to move you to a different health care facility. These decisions literally have life-or-death consequences. Make a wise decision and get it in writing now.

Durable Power of Attorney for Finances

Maybe you trust your family with your health care decisions but know that managing money can be a problem for them. Just like you may need someone to handle health care decisions, you will need someone you trust to be able to handle your financial affairs. This can involve paying ordinary bills such as your mortgage, signing legal documents, and even interacting with other entities on your behalf (like the phone company or your health insurance provider).

If you become incapacitated without this document in place, your spouse, relatives, or friends may have to go before a judge to get authority to handle your financial affairs.[19]

No one wants to have to jump through these hoops in the midst of what is already a difficult situation. Take care of this now so that you can know you will be in good hands, and your family members will be spared some stress during an already trying time.

A Living Will (Also Known as a Declaration, a Directive to Physicians, or a Health Care Directive)

If you are unwilling to turn over decision-making power regarding your health to anyone, you can set up a living will, which tells the doctors which procedures you would like provided or withheld in the event that you are unable to communicate such wishes yourself. Again, this alleviates stress for your loved ones, as your wishes are already stated clearly in writing.

---

19 If you don't have anyone like this in your life, many banks have trustees who can handle these affairs for a small fee.

Checklist 2: Estate Planning

The best things in life are free / But you can keep 'em for the
birds and bees / Now give me money (that's what I want).
—BARRETT STRONG, "Money (That's What I Want)"

When most people think of estate planning, they usually think of simply drafting a will. But there is much more to estate planning than just who gets what when you die. There are a number of different things you can do *today* that can help decrease your taxable income, and increase your tax efficiency. Here are the four core essentials.

Setting Up a Will. Drafting a will is the first step in any estate planning, and there are four key decisions you must make.

- Who are the beneficiaries? In other words, who gets what?
- Who will be the guardian for your children, if you have any children under the age of 18 when you pass away? If this isn't spelled out in a will, the courts get to determine who will raise your children. Let me say that again. The *courts* will get to decide who will raise *your* children! Are you paying attention yet?[20]
- Who will be the executor of the will? This is the person who will be in charge of making sure that what you request in your will actually happens, and the one dealing with probate if your estate must go through that process. (See the box that follows on why everyone should avoid probate regardless of how much money he or she has.)
- Do you want your assets distributed directly to the recipients or distributed to trusts set up on their behalf (a *testamentary trust*)? For example,

---

20 Sometimes the very people the court might likely choose (your parents or siblings) are not necessarily who *you* would choose to be guardians of your children. This is an important moment. Think about who in your family or even your close friends you trust to raise your children the way you would want them raised. What would provide your children with the most peace of mind after this tragedy? Talk about this with your spouse, determine who you'd like to choose, and then have the important conversation with them asking that they be listed as guardians.

let's say a couple has $400,000 in assets that will be split equally between their two children, who are currently ages 19 and 20, when they die. If the parents both pass today, the children will each get a check for $200,000 with no restrictions. What would you have done with $200,000 at age 19 or 20?[21] Instead, the parents could include a provision in their will for a testamentary trust that would allow their children to receive principal and income for their health and education until they are 30, at which point the balance of the trust will be distributed to them.[22] The will would also name a *testamentary trustee*, a person or company you select to hold the money, invest it, and distribute it in accordance with the terms of your testamentary trust.

WHAT IS PROBATE? AND WHY YOU SHOULD AVOID IT AT ALL COSTS

The main point of probate is to give your creditors time to seek payment of the money you owe them and your executor time to collect money owed to you. Probate involves payment of taxes and debts, and the distribution of what is left under court supervision. *What are the other downsides of probate?*

- **Control of Assets.** During the probate process, your beneficiaries cannot sell your assets; the executor can only sell assets only with the permission of the court.
- **Time.** The probate process takes approximately 6 months at a minimum, but it usually lasts at least a year. It can take even longer if matters become complicated by a will contest (where the validity of the will is challenged), business problems, or anything else unusual.[23]

21 If you are currently 19 or 20 with $200,000, may I suggest you revisit the investments chapter of this book?

22 I am convinced that 30 is the new 21.

23 The process can vary greatly depending on what state you live in.

- **Expenses.** It's possible for the costs of probate to stretch into the tens of thousands or even the *hundreds* of thousands for some estates.
- **Privacy.** Probate is a matter of public record, which means anyone can have access to your personal financial affairs. For many people, the thought of their most personal information being made public is pretty chilling. You may think that no one will be interested in your affairs; however, some people actually "work" probate records, looking for people who are going to inherit substantial sums of money in order to find ways to take advantage of them.

Trusts

A quick word on trusts: all too often, people assume that trusts are only for the Rockefellers and other 1-percenters, or something that you set up for your children should you pass away while they are still young. But I believe that trusts should be a centerpiece of estate planning for people with more modest assets as well. *They don't need to be expensive or complex to set up!*

One important responsibility we all have is to make sure that whatever wealth we build, however large or small it may be, our families benefit from it, and it doesn't get stuck in a legal process that drains the gift from our heirs. Trusts are an important tool to do just that. Read on to discover how to use them to your benefit. But first, a bit about tax planning.

Estate Tax Planning. As we discussed in chapter 6 on the Core Four, it's not necessarily about how much money you earn, it's about how much you keep. Tax efficiency is key to your financial freedom while you're alive, but you also have to consider what taxes you will incur upon your passing.

For most people, estate taxes are not and will never be a concern. Why? The IRS will allow you to give away up to $5.45 million over your lifetime or at your death without paying any taxes; this is referred to as your lifetime exemption. Think of it as a onetime coupon.[24] Married couples get to com-

24 Note: laws can change, as this is a political hot potato.

bine their lifetime-exemption amounts, so estate taxes are due only if their combined net worth exceeds $10.9 million.

If you are one of the wealthy that has more than $5.45 million to bestow upon your death, you will be paying an estate tax of 40%. Ouch! I hope you'll agree with me that it is worthwhile to discover ways to pass on some of your wealth now, before you pass away, so that you can decrease the amount of your taxable estate.

So, how can you do this? The IRS allows you to give away $14,000 per year to whomever you choose without counting against this lifetime exemption limit; this is referred to as your *annual exclusion*. Any amount over $14,000 is taxed at the gift rate of 40%. This means that you could give away $14,000 per person to all of your friends and family every year and still give away $5.45 million when you die, paying no gift or estate taxes on any of it. That can add up to quite a sum (depending on how many friends you actually have!).

Below are a few strategies for passing along your wealth without handing a huge chunk over to the government:

- **Help Pay for Your Children's or Grandchildren's College Education Expenses (and Get a Tax Benefit, Too!).** Most people don't realize that you can use part of your annual gift of $14,000 to fund a 529 college savings plan for your kids or grandchildren. You may even get a state income tax deduction for the gift as well. If the student is already attending college, tuition payments can be made *directly* to the school.
- **Instead of Waiting to Pass On Your Wealth After You Die, You Can Give $14,000 per Year Tax Free Directly to Each of Your Family Members.** Let's say you have grown kids who are married. You and your spouse can each give your child $14,000 per year, for a total of $28,000 annually. You can also each give your son-in-law or daughter-in-law $14,000 per year, for another $28,000. That means one married couple can give another married couple $56,000 per year with no *gift tax* consequences and without reducing your lifetime exemption! They get the benefit today, and you get the joy of sharing with your children while you're still alive.
- **Pay for Medical Expenses.** You can pay for the medical expenses of friends or family members without counting against your annual gifting limit, so

long as the payments are made *directly* to the care provider. So what does this mean? If your grandchild needs an emergency appendectomy (costing $20,000), you can cover those costs and still give that grandchild an additional $14,000 in the same year without paying the 40% gift tax.

- **Charitable Giving.** Any money you give to charitable organizations does not count toward the estate tax calculation either. Why pay it to the government when you can give it away? That's what the world's wealthiest have done, including Bill Gates and Warren Buffett. We cover this in more depth in checklist 4.

Revocable Living Trust. As you begin to accumulate wealth, please don't wait to set up a living trust. Everyone needs one. Why? *Because all assets in the trust avoid the complex state-run proceedings of probate.*

A revocable living trust is a simple, legal arrangement to hold assets (the *trust* part). Because this trust is put in place during your lifetime, it is a *living* trust. And because the trust is written to allow you to terminate the arrangement at any time, it's *revocable*. So even though the name looks confusing, revocable living trust just means "a legal arrangement created to hold your assets, which you can end any time you want while you're alive." You will be named as the *trustee* (or the person in charge of the assets), so you make whatever decisions you want with the assets in the trust. If you become incapacitated, or after you pass away, a *successor trustee* you name will take over the administration of the trust for you. And nothing touches probate!

> Ideas are a dime a dozen, and the implementation is everything.
> —JACK BOGLE

Protect Your Assets with an Irrevocable Trust. Some of the wealthiest families in the world have known for centuries what any great asset protection expert will tell you: the secret is to own nothing and control everything. This can be done through an *irrevocable trust*. It is considered to be a separate legal entity, so the assets inside it are not subject to estate tax when you die.[25] That's right, your family will keep that 40% rather

25 Assuming you set up and fund the trust more than three years before you die.

than see it confiscated by the government! Also, if the trust is established properly, the assets inside can be protected *while you are alive* from creditors, divorce, legal judgments, and other risks—thus its other name: an *asset protection trust*.[26] So what are the best ways to use an irrevocable trust to your advantage?[27]

- **Giving Annual Gifts.** As you learned a few pages ago, you are allowed to give an annual gift of $14,000 per person each year tax free. Rather than giving your annual gifts to your beneficiaries outright, it may make more sense to put that money in an irrevocable trust instead, and that person can be the beneficiary of the trust. This is particularly effective if a beneficiary is young, has difficulty managing money, or if there are extenuating circumstances that lead you to want to establish some benchmarks the person must achieve in order to obtain access to the funds, such as sobriety, attending college, or holding down a full-time job.
- **Holding Life Insurance.** Sheltering life insurance through the use of irrevocable trusts has become so common that this type of trust has acquired its own acronym: the *ILIT*, which stands for *irrevocable life insurance trust*. Most people know that the proceeds from a life insurance policy are not subject to income tax; however, it's not as widely known that the proceeds are subject to *estate* tax (that pesky 40%). However, if the policy is held within an irrevocable trust, you are able to avoid both income tax and estate tax! A double whammy. Here's how it works: you take the $14,000 annual gift ($14,000 per kid, per grandkid, if you want to contribute more) and use it to fund life insurance within an irrevocable trust, which allows your children or grandchildren to receive the life insurance payout completely tax free!

26 So what's the downside? Well, as its name states, it's irrevocable. Once the trust is established and funded, it's technically out of your control. In fact, you will name a trustee to make all decisions regarding how the funds are managed and distributed. However, you can also remove the trustee if necessary. Also, you can hire a professional, bonded trust company to do this for you.

27 Irrevocable trusts can also be used as part of other, more sophisticated planning strategies—such as advanced asset protection planning, providing support for family members with special needs, Medicaid planning, charitable gift planning, business sale planning—and much more.

- **For Ultra-High-Net-Worth Individuals, Use Your Lifetime Exemption Today.** Giving away a portion or all of your $5.45 million limit (or $10.9 million if you're married) today can be a great strategy, especially if given to a family member through an irrevocable trust for protection (for asset and tax protection). Why would anyone want to give away that much today? Let's say that you have certain assets valued at $5 million today that you expect to increase considerably in value over your lifetime: for example, shares of a company or a piece of undeveloped land. By giving the assets to the trust today, you pay no taxes on the transfer because it's under your lifetime exemption amount. *At your passing, hopefully decades later, the assets could have ballooned in value by that time.* If the original $5 million piece of land is now worth $20 million, the entire $20 million passes to the trust beneficiaries tax free.

Checklist 3: Insurance

Everyone's got a plan until they get punched in the mouth.
—MIKE TYSON

Many of the scenarios that can take you down financially can be covered with insurance. That's right, just like you insure your car because you don't want to be stuck with a bill in the thousands for a car accident that was just that (an accident), or how you pay for health insurance in case something catastrophic happens to your health, and you don't want hospital bills to cause you to go bankrupt, there are other kinds of insurance that can be a fantastic tool if wielded correctly. Listen, I get it: nobody likes insurance until he needs it. But you can do everything right—hire a fiduciary, reduce fees and taxes, construct an awesome portfolio—and in the blink of an eye, your efforts will be wiped out if you aren't prepared for a catastrophic loss.

So let's protect ourselves, shall we?

The fear of death follows from the fear of life. A man
who lives fully is prepared to die at any time.
—MARK TWAIN

Life Insurance. If you have insurance on your cell phone but not on your life, we need to talk. I'm not kidding. Life insurance is a crucial aspect to protecting your wealth and family. I have seen devastating situations where people with substantial means didn't have life insurance (or enough of it), and the family members quickly ran out of money when the income disappeared and the expenses piled up. So even if you have life insurance, let's take a look at the different types and make sure you have the right policy for you.

- **Term Insurance.** *Term insurance* is the most appropriate type of life insurance for nearly all Americans; however, term insurance is not often recommended by insurance agents, because selling it results in the lowest commission.[28] With a term insurance policy, you're insuring your life for a specific period of time (usually 10, 15, 20, or 30 years). At the end of the term, the policy ends, and you no longer have the coverage. Many insurance agents will use this as the reason that you should not buy term insurance: because you might never get a return on your investment. I find this to be quite a silly argument. It's like arguing that I should feel disappointed that I have homeowner's insurance and my home hasn't burned down! But term insurance can be helpful if you want to safeguard your family in case something happens to you before you have secured financial freedom. How long you need the coverage depends on how far off you are from your financial goals. An insurance agent, or your financial advisor, can help you determine those numbers.

- **Permanent Insurance.** As the name implies, you have this type of insurance for your entire life; thus, it's much more expensive because the insurance company is expecting to pay a death benefit at some point in the future. When is it a good idea to buy permanent insurance? As we discussed in the previous section, you can utilize permanent life insurance as part of your estate planning to both maximize your legacy and minimize your taxes by creating an irrevocable life insurance trust. You can also buy *survivorship life insurance* (also known as a second-to-die policy). This is a single policy covering the lives of two spouses or domestic partners. The policy pays out only

28 Remember our chapter on brokers? I could write a whole book on the ways the insurance industry tries to take advantage. But I digress . . .

after *both* insured individuals have passed. Because two lives are insured, the death benefit is greater than a policy would be on only one individual.[29] And remember, if held in an irrevocable trust, the proceeds will be free of income tax and estate tax!

- **Variable Life Insurance.** This is a kind of permanent life insurance, except the cash value is reinvested in a number of "subaccounts" that are similar to mutual funds. Watch out for these! These quasi "investment" vehicles are bogged down with fees, huge commissions, and actively managed funds. They also have high surrender charges if you want to get out. The only exception is a tool for the ultra-affluent called private placement life insurance (PPLI, or sometimes referred to as rich-man's Roth), where there is no commission paid, no surrender charges, and few limitations on the investments within. You probably haven't heard of it because life insurance agents can't make a dime selling it (and so it's usually structured by sophisticated attorneys). That said, private placement life insurance typically requires a deposit of $1 million or more, so it's truly a tool for those who have significant assets.[30]

HOW MUCH LIFE INSURANCE DO YOU REALLY NEED?

Determining how much life insurance you need should be an integral part of creating your financial plan and is something to be done with your financial advisor. There are many popular methodologies used to estimate how much life insurance a person needs. Most of them make no sense. For example, one popular rule of thumb is that you should purchase life insurance equivalent to five times your income. But when you think about it, if you make $100,000 per year and have $5 million, you likely don't need life insurance; the family will get by just fine. If you just graduated medical school with $250,000 in debt, purchased a $700,000 home, and have three little kids, then five times your income is likely nowhere near enough. Obviously,

29 You would purchase this kind of policy in order to maximize the value that a couple can gift each year tax free to fund the premiums for the policy. With those premiums, you typically buy as much death benefit as possible to maximize the proceeds.

30 Tony discusses the benefits of PPLI on page 446 of *MONEY Master the Game*.

the best method to determine how much you need is to customize the solution to *your* situation.

You'll need to reassess this number as you age, as you reach certain goals, or as you create new ones. For example, once your children are through college, or your mortgage is paid off, you no longer need to carry insurance to cover those liabilities, but you may need to keep saving for retirement. Again, this is when your financial advisor will earn his or her weight in gold.

> Time and health are two precious assets we don't recognize
> and appreciate until they have been depleted.
> —DENIS WAITLEY, speaker, writer, consultant

Disability Insurance. What do you think is your greatest asset? Many people think of their home or possibly their retirement account. For most, though, it's your ability to earn. Your goals for financial security and freedom are often dependent on your ability to keep the paychecks rolling in so that you can sock away enough to compound into a substantial nest egg. A disability could seriously derail all that you have set up.

Employers typically offer both short-term and long-term disability coverage for their employees, so it's a good idea to check what your employer offers before meeting with an insurance specialist.

"We've done everything we can do, Mr. Johnson.
Unfortunately, there is no cure for bad insurance."

Forty percent of individuals who reach age 65
will enter a nursing home during their lifetimes.

—MORNINGSTAR

Long-Term Care Insurance: Covering the Costs of Assisted Living.
Nobody likes to think about growing old. I understand. But unless you are
Benjamin Button, you have to make sure that if you someday need long-term
care, you have the necessary coverage. According to the *New York Times*: "Some
70% of those over age 65 will require some form of long-term care before
they die. But only about 20% have a long-term care insurance policy. Instead,
millions of those who end up needing long-term care pay for it out of pocket."

If you are fortunate enough to have a multimillion-dollar portfolio, a
properly structured portfolio would spin off the money needed to cover
your needs. However, the typical cost of a nursing home varies across the
country, from $67,525 per year in Des Moines, Iowa, to $168,630 per year
in New York City. Given that just 44% of the population over age 50 has
more than $100,000 in liquid assets, it shouldn't be much of a surprise that
most people who enter a nursing home are broke within a few years.

How do we prevent this? You need to get a long-term care policy for
yourself or those you love well before it's needed. You can, for example, purchase a policy that will cover $200 per day, or $72,800 per year, for up to 3
years, for a 65-year-old person for just $5,000 annually. However, if you wait
too long, it becomes cost prohibitive, and most insurance companies won't
insure people over the age of 84. Long-term care typically covers home care,
assisted living, adult day care, hospice, nursing home, and Alzheimer's facilities. Insurance policies like this are available for someone who is as young as
45 years old for as little as $100 per month.

Homeowner's Insurance. Our homes are one of our biggest assets, and
thus it makes sense to make sure that we are protected from certain things
beyond our control, such as a fire, tornado, earthquake, or flood. Homeowner's insurance protects you by covering the costs of damage to your home,
within the limits of your policy. (This is key. Often we don't fully understand
the limits and conditions of these policies and then find ourselves stuck with
bills we never expected to pay.)

As with all insurance, your first step should be to determine exactly how much coverage you need. This requires you to evaluate the *replacement* value of your home, which can be different from the sales price of your home. Your *dwelling coverage* should match what it would cost to rebuild your home from the ground up, using the same or similar materials. In some areas of the country, the cost of materials has continued to go up while real estate values have remained level, so it's important to understand what current building costs are and to calculate your dwelling coverage appropriately. However, it's important to note that your insurance company will *fully* cover damages to your home *only* if your dwelling coverage is at least 80% of the replacement value of your home. What does that mean? Let's say you own a home valued at $500,000, and your dwelling coverage is $350,000. If one of your water pipes bursts, causing $50,000 in damage, even though your dwelling coverage more than covers the $50,000 in damage, the insurance company is going to send you a check for $43,750 (minus any deductible) and not $50,000.[31]

Many people are surprised to discover that their policies do not provide as much coverage as they think, because of internal caps on how much damage is covered by the policy or payout limitations for valuable articles. For this reason, it often makes sense for individuals with high-value homes, rental properties, or other valuable or unique properties (yachts, collectors vehicles, and so forth) to work with specialty insurers selling products designed to protect these types of assets, so that you don't find yourself paying for insurance that ultimately doesn't protect you the way you thought.

Umbrella Insurance. If your umbrella is not insured, you might be required to replace it if a windstorm rolls in. (I'm sorry, I'm just kidding. Writing about insurance is making me delirious.) An *umbrella policy* is an excess-liability policy that covers you above and beyond the liability limits of

---

31 The insurance company uses a ratio of the amount of coverage you actually have (in this example, 70% of the replacement value) compared with the amount of coverage you should have (80% of the replacement value of your home). $350,000/$400,000 = 87.5%, so they will cover 87.5% of the $50,000 claim, or $43,750.

your home and auto policies. *It's effectively an asset protection policy that covers all sorts of things that can happen any time and for any reason, often unfolding in ways we couldn't imagine.* We live in an increasingly litigious society and the parents of that kid down the street might sue you if he gets hurt jumping on your trampoline. We may do everything in our power to secure our financial independence, but none of that would matter if we lost a big lawsuit. For this reason, it makes sense for many of us to have an umbrella policy. When we purchase an umbrella policy, we are also purchasing the ability to access the team of attorneys that works for the insurance company, in the hopes that any liability issues that may come up will be settled by this team.

Checklist 4: Leaving a Legacy

There is one thing in common among all the titans Tony interviewed: they not only love to earn money for themselves and their families but also love to give it away. They know firsthand the joy that comes from sharing wealth with causes that are important and mean something to them. Remember, one of the reasons that Tony and I wrote this book is to help feed a billion people!

However, when most people think of donating, they think of writing a check to their favorite charity or cause. *But in the section that follows, I'll suggest the best ways to share your wealth with these causes while also increasing your tax efficiency.* Below are a few ways you can *truly* maximize your impact:

- **Leave the Right Assets to Charity.** Many times, individuals name their children as the beneficiaries of their IRA or retirement account, and they specify a bequest of cash or other property to a charity. This isn't always the best solution. For example, if you leave a traditional IRA valued at $100,000 to your children and a piece of land valued at $100,000 to a charity, your children will have to pay taxes on the distributions from the IRA. If, instead, you leave the IRA to a charity and the land to your children, the charity can cash out the IRA with no tax consequences, and your children can sell the property at your death without paying taxes either.

  Here's another example: let's say that Mrs. Donor owned some Microsoft stock that she bought ages ago. If she sold it, she would have to pay significant capital gains tax. However, if the stock is donated, the donor avoids ever having to pay capital gains tax, doesn't have to part with cash, and still gets the tax deduction for giving to a charity of her choice.

- **Work with a Donor-Advised Fund.** A *donor-advised fund* is a public charity that has two primary functions. First, it will help you find organizations that are making a meaningful difference in areas in which you have an interest. Second, when you donate to a donor-advised fund, it will segregate those donations into a separate account that is yours to direct. It's kind of like your own private charity. So if you donate $25,000 to a donor-advised fund, first, you get an immediate tax deduction. Then, at your leisure, you can direct those funds to different charities as you see fit.

- **Establish a Private Foundation.** For ultra-high-net-worth individuals, creating your own private foundation can be a great way to create a multigenerational charitable legacy. A *private foundation* is an independent charitable entity with a staff and directors who administer the operations of the foundation and the distribution of assets to support the mission. While there are more rules and regulations regarding the use and distribution of funds from a private foundation—which, along with staffing needs, can make it more expensive to operate—family members can be paid a salary for their work with the foundation.

- **Look for Creative Ways to Increase Your Impact.** A number of companies are creating exponential impact in the field of charitable giving using crowdsourcing. For example, Crowdrise (www.crowdrise.com) was cofounded by actor Edward Norton and has exploded into the top 25 global philanthropies, according to *Barron's* (Tony was one of its initial investors). Given new technologies and large social networks, Crowdrise has a unique approach for creating maximum impact: a friendly competition among charities that want your donation. Let's say that you wanted to donate $100K to a charity focused on clean water. Crowdrise will approach ten (or more) different clean-water charities to compete for your donation. For 1 month, the competing charities will go to their own donor network, letting them know that whoever raises the most money in the month will win this $100K grant. If each charity raises $50K on average (10 charities x $50K = $500K), and the winner also gets your $100K, a total of $600K was raised—$500K more than you donated personally!

And Here's Your Diploma!

If you have made it to this page, congratulations! You have now not only determined how to become unshakeable in building your wealth, but also learned exactly what you need to do to protect your family, reduce your taxes, and leave a legacy of giving. It may take a few conversations with your lawyer, your financial advisor, and your insurance specialist. A little bit of focus today can provide invaluable peace of mind for you and your family.

INDEX

disability insurance, 216
discipline, 145
diversification, 49, 109–12, 126, 135,
    137, 151, 153–54, 158
    four types of, 110
    international, 157–58
    risk/reward and, 99, 111–12,
    126–27
    within asset classes, 135–36
donor-advised funds, 220
Dow Jones Industrial Average, 149
Druckenmiller, Stanley, 144
dually registered advisors, 81–83
durable power of attorney:
    for finances, 206
    for health care, 205

Edison International, 70
electroencephalograms and
    electrocardiograms, 179–80
emotional and mental states:
    beautiful, 170–72, 175–78, 183, 185
    suffering, see suffering
emotional wealth, 163–87
emotions, 17–20, 122, 126, 145, 149,
    161, 174, 178
    fear, see fear
    happiness, 18, 163, 167, 168, 170,
    171, 173, 175, 176, 178, 180
    wealth and, 163
endorphins, 155, 156
endowment effect, 147
energy investments, 107, 108, 132
energy-rich and energy-poor states,
    170
Erdoes, Mary Callahan, 9, 111
ERISA (Employee Retirement
    Income Security Act), 63
estate planning, 202–13
    probate and, see probate

taxes and, 209–11, 212
    will in, see will
events, mistaking for trends, 148–52
exchange-traded funds, 14
expectations, 148–50, 173, 175
experts, 29–30, 127
    predictions by, 31–35, 50, 156
extraordinary quality of life, 164–65,
    167, 168, 170, 175
ExxonMobil, 52

Fast Company, 57
fear, 10–11, 18–20, 46, 119–20, 124,
    159, 161, 172, 180
    of bear markets, 11, 16, 18, 27,
    137
    facts to free you from, see
    Freedom Facts
    loss aversion and, 158–61
Federal Reserve, 103
Feeding America, 10, 109, 219
fees, 14–15, 17, 46, 47–48, 53, 55–56,
    59–60, 75, 76, 153, 155
    brokers and, 84
    categories of, 62–63
    commissions, 17, 85, 214
    consulting, 85
    expense ratio in, 54
    in 401(k) plans, 47, 61–70
    front-end load, 65
    hidden, 54, 62
    ignorance about, 47–48, 62
    impact of, 63
    model portfolios and, 84–85
    for selecting investments, 84–85
    transaction costs, 50–51, 52, 54, 153
Fidelity, 91
fiduciaries, 76, 79, 81–83, 85–86,
    90, 91
50 Cent, 23